U

FACIAL SHAPING WORKOUT

for Women

Lift Your Face, Reduce **Double Chin** and **Face Fat**, and Boost Your Confidence with **Quick and Easy Routines**

Tessa Grimes

Disclaimer

The information provided in this book is for educational and informational purposes only and is not intended as medical advice. The recipes and meal plans in this book are designed to support healthy eating habits, but they should not be considered as a substitute for professional medical advice, diagnosis, or treatment.

Before making any changes to your diet, it is important to consult with a healthcare provider.

Every effort has been made to ensure the recipes and nutritional information in this book are accurate, but variations in ingredients, preparation methods, and individual dietary needs may result in different outcomes. Always check the nutritional content of packaged foods and follow your healthcare provider's advice.

The author and publisher of this book are not responsible for any adverse effects or consequences resulting from the use of any recipe, suggestion, or product mentioned in this book.

TABLE OF CONTENTS

Introduction

Journey to a Defined Jawline

What to Expect from This Book

This book is designed to be your guide in achieving a more defined jawline, a slimmer chin, and ultimately, a boost in confidence through the power of facial exercises. With a focus on simplicity and effectiveness, the routines outlined here are crafted to fit seamlessly into your busy lifestyle, ensuring that you can work towards your beauty goals without the need for invasive procedures or expensive treatments. By engaging in these carefully selected exercises, you will learn how to sculpt your face, reduce the appearance of double chin fat, and tone your facial muscles, all of which contribute to a more youthful and radiant appearance.

The exercises we will explore are based on the principles of muscle engagement and toning, similar to how you would tone any other part of your body. However, the muscles of your face and neck are unique in their structure and function, requiring specialized routines to effectively target them. This book breaks down the science behind facial exercises, providing you with a clear understanding of how consistent practice can improve the tone, elasticity, and contour of your face.

As you embark on this journey, remember that technique and consistency are key. The routines are designed to be quick and easy, allowing for integration into your daily life without significant time investment. Whether you're watching TV, driving, or doing chores, there's an opportunity to engage in these exercises. By committing to the 28-Day Challenge included in this book, you will not only see visible results but also develop a habit that can be continued beyond the challenge period for long-term benefits.

Our goal is to empower you with the knowledge and tools needed to take control of your facial aesthetics. Through dedication and consistent practice, you will discover the transformative power of facial exercises, leading to not just a more defined facial structure but also an enhanced sense of self-confidence.

Why Facial Exercises Work

Facial exercises are grounded in the principles of muscle toning and engagement, akin to workouts designed for other parts of the body. The unique aspect of facial workouts lies in their ability to specifically target the muscles beneath the skin's surface, which play a pivotal role in shaping the contours of the face. Over time, these muscles can lose their tone and elasticity due to a variety of factors including aging, lack of use, and environmental stressors. This loss of tone and elasticity often leads to sagging skin, a less defined jawline, and the appearance of a double chin. By engaging in targeted facial exercises, individuals can effectively counteract these effects by strengthening the muscles, thereby restoring their natural elasticity and firmness.

The science behind why facial exercises work is rooted in the body's natural response to muscle conditioning. When facial muscles are exercised regularly, blood circulation to the area increases, which enhances oxygen supply and nutrient delivery to the skin cells and muscle fibers. This improved circulation not only helps to tone and firm the muscles but also contributes to a healthier, more radiant complexion. Additionally, consistent muscle engagement helps to build muscle fiber size, which can add volume to facial contours, creating a more youthful appearance.

Another key aspect of facial exercises is their ability to promote collagen production. Collagen is a protein that plays a crucial role in maintaining skin elasticity and firmness. As we age, collagen production naturally declines, leading to wrinkles and sagging skin. Regular facial muscle stimulation through exercises can signal the body to increase collagen production, helping to mitigate the visible signs of aging.

Moreover, facial exercises offer a natural and non-invasive solution to sculpting the face and reducing unwanted fat. Unlike surgical procedures or cosmetic treatments, which can be costly and carry risks of complications, facial exercises can be performed at home without any special equipment. This accessibility makes it an appealing option for many individuals seeking to improve their facial aesthetics.

It's important to note that while facial exercises are effective, results are not instantaneous. Just as with any form of exercise, consistency and patience are key. Over time, as the facial muscles become stronger and more toned, individuals will begin to notice improvements in their facial structure, including a more defined jawline, reduced double chin, and overall facial slimming. The key to achieving these results lies in the regular and correct execution of facial exercises, ensuring that each muscle group is engaged properly to maximize benefits.

Incorporating facial exercises into one's daily routine can be a simple yet powerful way to enhance facial aesthetics and boost confidence. By dedicating just a few minutes each day to these exercises, individuals can take proactive steps towards maintaining a youthful and vibrant appearance, demonstrating the effectiveness and value of facial muscle engagement in achieving long-term facial contouring and skin health benefits.

Technique and Consistency for Lasting Results

Mastering the art of facial exercises requires a keen focus on technique and a steadfast commitment to consistency. The journey to a more defined jawline and a reduction in facial fat is not a quick fix but a gradual process that unfolds over time. The precision with which each exercise is performed plays a pivotal role in targeting the muscles effectively, ensuring that the effort invested translates into visible results. Proper technique ensures that each facial muscle is engaged correctly, maximizing the benefits of the exercises without risking strain or injury. It's akin to sculpting, where every detail matters, and precision shapes the outcome.

Consistency is the bedrock of success in any fitness endeavor, and facial exercises are no exception. The human body thrives on regularity, and the facial muscles respond positively to consistent stimulation. Engaging in facial exercises daily creates a routine that the body begins to anticipate and respond to more effectively over time. This consistent effort reinforces muscle memory, gradually enhancing muscle tone and strength. It's important to integrate these exercises into daily routines, making them as habitual as brushing teeth or applying skincare. This integration ensures that the exercises are not viewed as an additional task but as a natural part of one's self-care regimen.

The transformative power of facial exercises unfolds over time, with patience being a critical component of the process.

Immediate results should not be the expectation; rather, the focus should be on the incremental improvements that cumulate into significant changes. Just as a seed requires time to sprout and grow, the benefits of facial exercises build gradually, revealing a more toned and defined facial structure as time progresses. This journey is not measured in days but in the dedication shown over weeks and months. The commitment to daily practice, even when results are not immediately visible, is what leads to lasting changes.

It's also crucial to approach this practice with a mindset geared towards long-term maintenance rather than a temporary fix. The goal is to cultivate a routine that can be sustained over the long haul, ensuring that the results achieved are not fleeting but are a permanent enhancement to one's facial aesthetics. This long-term perspective fosters a deeper appreciation for the process and the subtle yet significant transformations that occur.

In essence, the effectiveness of facial exercises is significantly influenced by the attention paid to technique and the commitment to consistent practice. These elements are the foundation upon which the journey to a more defined jawline and reduced facial fat is built. By embracing these principles, individuals can unlock the full potential of facial exercises, achieving results that are not only visible but also lasting. The path to facial rejuvenation is one of patience, precision, and persistence, leading to a destination where confidence and satisfaction in one's appearance are profoundly enhanced.

Integrating Exercises into Daily Life

Incorporating facial exercises into your daily routine is a seamless way to ensure you're consistently working towards a more defined jawline and reduced facial fat, even amidst a busy schedule. The beauty of these exercises is their flexibility; they can be done anywhere, at any time, without requiring special equipment or significant chunks of your day. Here are practical tips on how to integrate facial exercises into activities you're already doing, turning routine tasks into opportunities for enhancing your facial aesthetics.

While watching TV, a time many use to unwind, you can also engage in facial toning. Sit comfortably and maintain good posture, then perform jaw juts or chin lifts during commercials. These exercises require minimal movement but yield significant results over time. The repetitive nature of TV commercials offers a perfect, timed interval for performing these exercises, making it easy to complete several sets without missing your favorite show.

Driving presents another prime opportunity for facial workouts. While stopped at traffic lights or in heavy traffic, practice the tongue stretch by reaching the tongue to the roof of your mouth as far as possible, then pressing it flat against the roof to engage the muscles under your chin. This exercise can help in reducing double chin and tightening the neck muscles. Always ensure you're fully focused on driving and that conditions are safe for multitasking.

Chores such as doing the dishes or laundry can be monotonous but turning them into a chance to work on your facial muscles can make them more productive. Opt for the ceiling pout or cheek lifts while engaged in these tasks. Simply tilt your head back to look at the ceiling, pout your lips as if blowing a kiss, and hold the position to stretch and tone your neck and lower facial muscles. These exercises can be easily integrated into moments where your hands are busy, but your face is free.

Remember, the key to seeing results from facial exercises is consistency. By integrating these exercises into your daily activities, you're more likely to stick with them long-term. It's about making the most of the time you have, turning vvotherwise idle moments into productive sessions for your facial fitness. Over time, these moments add up, contributing significantly to your journey towards a more defined jawline and a reduction in facial fat. The goal is to make facial exercises a natural and effortless part of your daily life, just like any other self-care habit. By doing so, you not only work towards enhancing your physical appearance but also embrace a lifestyle that prioritizes personal well-being and confidence.

BONUS EXTRA

Scan the QR CODE

and Get Your Free Access to 5-Minute Video Routines, The Ultimate Guide to Facial Lymphatic Drainage, and 28-Day Facial Shaping Challenge!

Elevate your facial fitness journey with these exclusive bonuses

bitly

As SPAM Filters Are Pretty Crazy These Days...
...WHITELIST this Email Address!

info@pureharmonypublishing.com

In This Way, Your Bonus Will Appear in the Main Folder of Your INBOX and They Will Not Be Buried Along With Other Advertisements in Your PROMOTION/SPAM Folder.

HERE IS HOW TO DO IT:

From Android Smartphone/Tablet
Open the Contacts App;
In the lower right corner, tap + (Add);
Enter the name and email address and then tap Save.

From iPhone/iPad
Open the Contacts App;
In the upper right corner, tap + (Add);
Enter the name and email address and then tap Finish.

Chapter 1

Muscles of Face and Neck

Key Muscles for Toned Jawline and Neck

The foundation of a sculpted jawline and a graceful neck lies in understanding the intricate network of muscles that shape this area. The key players in defining the contours of the face and neck include the masseter, temporalis, medial pterygoid, and lateral pterygoid muscles, which together are responsible for the movement of the jaw. The platysma, a broad sheet of muscle extending from the chest up to the jawline, plays a crucial role in the appearance of the neck and the lower face. Additionally, the sternocleidomastoid muscles, which extend along the sides of the neck, are vital for neck flexibility and posture, significantly influencing the overall aesthetics of the neck and jawline.

The masseter, one of the strongest muscles in the body, is pivotal for chewing and jaw clenching. Its tone and volume directly impact the width and definition of the lower face, contributing to a more pronounced jawline. The temporalis muscle, spanning the side of the head, assists in elevating the jaw and plays a role in the side contour of the face. The medial and lateral pterygoid muscles, though less visible, are essential for the complex movements of the jaw, including grinding and side-to-side motion, affecting the lower face's overall shape and function.

The platysma, often overlooked in discussions of facial aesthetics, is instrumental in the appearance of the neck and the lower jaw. As we age, the platysma can become lax, contributing to the appearance of sagging skin and the dreaded "turkey neck." Engaging and toning this muscle through targeted exercises can help tighten the skin of the neck and define the jawline, offering a non-surgical solution to maintaining a youthful profile.

The sternocleidomastoid muscles, running from the collarbone and sternum up to the ear, are key to neck posture and movement. Well-toned sternocleidomastoid muscles contribute to a swan-like neck, enhancing the overall elegance of the neck and jawline. These muscles also play a role in the angle between the neck and the jaw, which is crucial for the perception of a firm, youthful appearance.

Understanding the role of these muscles is the first step in crafting an effective facial exercise regimen. By targeting these muscles with specific exercises, it's possible to enhance muscle tone, improve skin tightness, and redistribute fat more favorably. This, in turn, leads to a more defined jawline, a slimmer chin, and a firmer neck, contributing significantly to the facial structure's overall firmness and appearance. Engaging in a routine that includes exercises for these key muscles can not only sculpt the face but also offer the added benefit of improving posture and breathing, which further enhances the aesthetic results.

The impact of these muscles on facial structure, firmness, and appearance cannot be overstated. A well-defined jawline and a toned neck are hallmarks of youth and beauty, and with the right approach, achieving these features is within reach. Through consistent practice, dedication to technique, and a deeper understanding of the underlying muscular anatomy, individuals can unlock the potential for significant improvements in their facial aesthetics, boosting confidence and radiance from the inside out.

Muscle Tone and Skin Tightness

The intricate relationship between muscle tone, skin tightness, and fat distribution is foundational to understanding how facial aesthetics can be enhanced through exercise. Stronger muscles play a pivotal role in supporting the skin, much like a well-constructed scaffold supports a building, ensuring that it maintains its shape and integrity over time. As muscle tone improves, it acts as a natural tightening agent, pulling the skin closer and reducing the appearance of sagging. This effect is particularly noticeable in the face and neck, where the skin is more delicate and prone to the visible signs of aging. Enhanced muscle tone beneath the skin's surface compresses fat cells and redistributes them more evenly, contributing to a smoother, more contoured appearance. This redistribution of fat cells is crucial in areas prone to fat accumulation, such as under the chin, where it can create a double chin effect. By engaging in targeted facial exercises, you can activate and strengthen the muscles in this area, leading to a more defined jawline and a reduction in the appearance of a double chin.

Moreover, the act of strengthening these muscles does more than just improve physical appearance; it also boosts blood circulation to the face. Increased blood flow enriches the skin with oxygen and vital nutrients, which are essential for maintaining skin elasticity and promoting a healthy, radiant complexion. This improved circulation further supports the skin's natural repair processes, helping to slow the signs of aging and reduce the likelihood of sagging and wrinkles. It's a virtuous cycle: as muscles become more toned, the skin becomes firmer and more resilient, and fat is more effectively distributed, all of which contribute to a youthful and vibrant appearance.

It's important to recognize that while the benefits of improved muscle tone are significant, they don't occur overnight. Just as with any exercise regimen, consistency is key. Incorporating facial exercises into your daily routine ensures that the muscles of the face and neck remain active and engaged, preventing the atrophy that can lead to sagging and uneven fat distribution. These exercises are designed to be seamlessly integrated into your lifestyle, requiring no special equipment and minimal time commitment, making them an ideal solution for the busy, health-conscious individual.

To maximize the benefits of facial exercises, focus on routines that target the major muscle groups of the face and neck. Exercises that emphasize the jawline, cheeks, and forehead can help to create a balanced approach to muscle strengthening, ensuring that all areas of the face benefit from increased tone and tightness. As you become more adept at these exercises, you can adjust the intensity and duration to continue challenging your muscles, ensuring ongoing improvements in tone, tightness, and fat distribution.

Remember, the goal of these exercises is not just to enhance your physical appearance but also to promote overall facial health. By dedicating time to strengthen the muscles of your face and neck, you're investing in a natural, non-invasive method of maintaining your youthful appearance, boosting your confidence, and enhancing your well-being. The journey to a more toned, firm, and contoured face is one that requires patience, dedication, and a commitment to self-care, but the rewards are well worth the effort. Through consistent practice, you can achieve lasting results that not only transform your appearance but also reflect your inner health and vitality.

Causes of Double Chin and Facial Sagging

The development of a double chin and facial sagging can be attributed to several factors, each playing a significant role in the changing contours of the face and neck. Understanding these causes is crucial for anyone looking to address these common concerns through facial exercises and lifestyle adjustments.

Fat accumulation under the chin, known as submental fat, is a primary contributor to the appearance of a double chin. This can occur due to weight gain, but it's also a natural part of aging as the skin loses its elasticity and the distribution of fat in the body changes. As we age, our metabolic rate slows down, which can lead to an increase in fat deposits in various parts of the body, including the area under the chin. This accumulation of fat can create a fuller appearance in the lower face and diminish the definition between the neck and jawline.

Genetics also play a significant role in determining the structure and appearance of our face and neck. Some individuals are genetically predisposed to have more fat cells in the submental area or have a weaker chin and jawline structure, which can make them more susceptible to developing a double chin. Additionally, genetic factors can influence how our skin ages, including how quickly it loses elasticity and how fat is distributed across the face. These inherited traits can make it more challenging for some to maintain a defined jawline and tight skin on the neck and face without intervention.

Poor posture is another critical factor contributing to facial sagging and the development of a double chin. Spending long hours in front of a computer or looking down at a smartphone encourages the neck to bend forward, weakening the neck and jawline muscles over time. This forward posture can lead to the shortening and weakening of the neck muscles, contributing to sagging skin and a less defined jawline. The constant downward angle can also cause the skin to lose its elasticity faster, as it's not being supported or stretched in a way that maintains its firmness.

Addressing these causes requires a multifaceted approach. Incorporating targeted facial exercises can help tone the muscles of the face and neck, improving muscle strength and skin elasticity, which can reduce the appearance of a double chin and sagging. Adjusting lifestyle habits, such as improving posture and maintaining a healthy weight, can also have a significant impact. For posture improvement, being mindful of keeping the head aligned over the spine and regularly engaging in exercises that strengthen the back and neck muscles can help. Additionally, a balanced diet rich in nutrients supports skin health and can prevent excessive fat accumulation.

While genetics may set a baseline for our facial structure and how our skin ages, proactive measures like facial exercises, lifestyle adjustments, and posture correction can make a tangible difference. These efforts can help mitigate the effects of genetics and aging, allowing for a more defined jawline and firmer facial appearance. Engaging in a consistent routine that targets the muscles of the face and neck, alongside healthy lifestyle choices, offers a natural and effective way to combat the common concerns of a double chin and facial sagging, empowering individuals to enhance their appearance and confidence without invasive procedures.

Posture and Breathing for Muscle Activation

Proper posture and breathing are foundational elements that significantly impact the effectiveness of facial exercises, directly influencing the activation of muscles in the face and neck. When engaging in facial shaping workouts, the alignment of the spine and the manner in which breath is controlled play a crucial role in ensuring that the targeted muscles are engaged optimally. This engagement is essential for achieving the desired outcomes of a defined jawline, reduced double chin, and overall facial toning.

Starting with posture, maintaining a straight spine with shoulders relaxed but aligned over the hips allows for the muscles in the neck and face to stretch and contract more effectively. This alignment ensures that exercises targeting the lower face and neck, such as chin lifts or neck stretches, are performed with maximum efficiency. The correct posture acts as a stable foundation, enabling precise muscle engagement and preventing unnecessary strain on surrounding muscles that could lead to uneven toning or even injury.

Breathing, on the other hand, is not merely a background process but a dynamic part of facial exercises. Controlled breathing not only oxygenates the muscles, enhancing their endurance and resilience during workouts but also helps in rhythmically coordinating the exercises for better results. For instance, inhaling deeply before an exercise and exhaling on the exertion can increase the intensity of the muscle engagement, thereby amplifying the benefits of each movement. Furthermore, focused breathing helps in maintaining a relaxed state during the exercises, which is vital to prevent the formation of tension-related wrinkles and to promote a more youthful appearance.

Incorporating proper posture and breathing techniques into facial exercises ensures that each movement is as effective as possible. By aligning the body correctly, the muscles in the face and neck are primed for optimal activation, allowing for more pronounced and quicker results from the workout. Similarly, by harnessing the power of breath, not only is the effectiveness of the exercises enhanced, but it also contributes to a holistic approach to wellness that transcends mere physical appearance.

To integrate these principles into your facial exercise routine, start by assessing your posture before each exercise, making adjustments to ensure your spine is straight, and your shoulders are relaxed. During the exercises, focus on your breathing, ensuring you are inhaling and exhaling fully and in a controlled manner, synchronizing your breath with your movements. This mindful approach to posture and breathing will not only improve the outcomes of your facial shaping workouts but also contribute to a greater sense of well-being and confidence in your appearance.

Chapter 2

Fundamentals of Facial Exercises

Correct Posture and Breathing Techniques

Maintaining a straight spine is the cornerstone of correct posture during facial exercises, ensuring that the shoulders are relaxed yet aligned directly over the hips to optimize the engagement of facial and neck muscles. This alignment is crucial for performing exercises aimed at the lower face and neck, such as chin lifts or neck stretches, with maximum efficiency. A stable foundation provided by correct posture enables precise muscle engagement, which is essential for achieving the desired outcomes of a defined jawline, reduced double chin, and overall facial toning without causing unnecessary strain on surrounding muscles that could lead to uneven toning or injury.

Breathing techniques play an equally vital role in the effectiveness of facial exercises. Controlled breathing not only oxygenates the muscles, enhancing their endurance and resilience during workouts but also assists in rhythmically coordinating the exercises for improved results. For example, taking a deep breath before starting an exercise and exhaling upon exertion can significantly increase muscle engagement intensity, thereby amplifying the benefits of each movement. Moreover, focused breathing aids in maintaining a relaxed state during the exercises, crucial for preventing tension-related wrinkles and promoting a more youthful appearance.

To seamlessly integrate these principles into your facial exercise routine, begin by assessing your posture before initiating any exercise, making necessary adjustments to ensure your spine is straight and your shoulders are relaxed. Throughout the exercises, concentrate on your breathing, making sure you are inhaling and exhaling fully in a controlled manner, and synchronize your breath with your movements. This mindful approach to posture and breathing not only enhances the outcomes of your facial shaping workouts but also contributes to a greater sense of well-being and confidence in your appearance.

By aligning the body correctly, the muscles in the face and neck are primed for optimal activation, allowing for more pronounced and quicker results from the workout. Similarly, harnessing the power of breath not only enhances the effectiveness of the exercises but also fosters a holistic approach to wellness that transcends mere physical appearance. This comprehensive strategy ensures that each movement in your facial exercise routine is as effective as possible, leading to more significant and satisfying results in your journey toward a more defined and youthful facial appearance.

Proper Warm-Up for Optimal Results

Just as athletes prepare their bodies for a workout with a series of stretches and light exercises to prevent injury and enhance performance, engaging in a proper warm-up routine is crucial before starting facial exercises. This preparatory step is essential for increasing blood circulation to the face, which nourishes the skin cells with oxygen and vital nutrients, leading to a radiant complexion. Additionally, warming up the facial muscles helps to increase their elasticity, which is vital for performing the exercises effectively and safely, reducing the risk of strain or injury.

To begin, focus on boosting circulation with gentle tapping all over the face using the fingertips. This action not only awakens the skin but also stimulates blood flow, preparing the muscles for more targeted movements. Start from the forehead, gradually moving to the cheeks, and then down to the jawline and neck. This technique not only invigorates the skin but also helps to relieve any tension held in the facial muscles, promoting relaxation and readiness for the exercises ahead.

Following the tapping, proceed with a series of facial stretches to enhance flexibility. Open the mouth wide, as if yawning, to stretch the jaw and neck muscles, holding the position for a few seconds before releasing. Repeat this movement several times to ensure the muscles are adequately loosened. Next, perform exaggerated smile and frown movements to stretch the cheek muscles, holding each expression for a few seconds. These expressions not only stretch the muscles but also contribute to a greater range of motion during the exercises.

Incorporate eye exercises by looking up, down, and side to side without moving your head. This movement helps to strengthen the eye muscles and increase blood flow around the eyes, reducing puffiness and improving overall eye health. Finish the warm-up with neck rotations, gently turning the head from side to side and tilting it forward and backward. This not only stretches the neck muscles but also aligns the spine, ensuring proper posture, which is a foundational aspect of effective facial exercises.

This warm-up routine, taking just a few minutes, is a vital step in the facial exercise regimen. It prepares the face and neck for the exercises by increasing circulation, enhancing flexibility, and ensuring the muscles are ready for the targeted movements that follow. By incorporating these simple warm-up exercises into your daily routine, you can maximize the effectiveness of your facial workouts, leading to more pronounced and quicker results. Engaging in this preparatory step demonstrates a commitment to the health and well-being of your skin and facial muscles, setting the stage for a successful facial shaping workout.

Chapter 3

Double Chin Reduction Exercises

Understanding Double Chin Formation and Fat Reduction

The formation of a double chin is primarily due to the accumulation of submental fat, which sits just beneath the chin. While weight gain is a common cause, other factors such as genetics, aging, and lifestyle choices can also contribute to the development of a double chin. For instance, as we age, our skin loses its natural elasticity, and the muscles that support the neck and chin weaken, resulting in sagging skin and fat deposits becoming more visible. Poor posture, such as slouching or craning the neck forward, can also exacerbate the appearance of a double chin by putting strain on the muscles of the neck and jaw, leading to further sagging.

In addition to the impact of aging and lifestyle factors, some individuals may be predisposed to developing a double chin due to genetic factors, which can affect where the body tends to store fat. This means that even individuals at a healthy weight might still struggle with excess fat under the chin. While it is impossible to directly control where the body loses fat, incorporating targeted muscle activation exercises can significantly improve the appearance of the neck and chin area. Strengthening the muscles around the jawline and neck can help tighten the skin, enhance definition, and contribute to a more sculpted and toned look.

To achieve effective fat reduction in this area, it is essential to adopt a holistic approach that combines facial exercises with overall fat loss through proper nutrition and regular physical activity. Consistency in practicing double chin reduction exercises is key to long-term success. By understanding the underlying factors contributing to double chin formation and applying consistent effort, you can gradually reduce submental fat and achieve a more defined, youthful appearance.

How Submental Fat Develops

Submental fat, commonly referred to as a double chin, accumulates under the chin and around the neck, creating a fuller appearance that can affect the overall contour and definition of the jawline. This accumulation of fat is influenced by several factors, including genetics, weight gain, aging, and posture. Genetics play a pivotal role in determining the distribution of fat within our bodies, including the facial structure. Some individuals are predisposed to store more fat under their chin due to their genetic makeup, making them more likely to develop a double chin even if they maintain a healthy weight. Weight gain is another significant factor contributing to the development of submental fat. As the body stores excess calories as fat, it can deposit in various areas, including under the chin, leading to increased fullness in that region. This is why weight management through diet and exercise is often recommended as a strategy for reducing the appearance of a double chin.

Aging also impacts the appearance of submental fat due to the natural loss of skin elasticity and muscle tone over time. As we age, the skin and muscles under the chin may sag, making any accumulated fat more noticeable. This process is exacerbated by the body's decreasing ability to produce collagen and elastin, compounds that contribute to the skin's firmness and elasticity. Furthermore, poor posture, especially from prolonged periods of looking down at mobile devices or computers, can weaken the neck and chin muscles. This weakening can lead to a reduction in the support structure for the skin, potentially accentuating the appearance of a double chin by allowing the skin to droop and fat to appear more prominent.

Addressing submental fat and its contributing factors requires a multifaceted approach. Engaging in regular physical activity and maintaining a balanced diet can help manage overall body weight and potentially reduce the appearance of a double chin. Facial exercises targeting the neck and chin area may also be beneficial by toning the muscles, thereby providing better support for the skin and creating a more defined jawline. Additionally, improving posture, especially while using electronic devices, can help strengthen the neck and chin muscles, reducing the likelihood of sagging skin and accumulated fat in the area. While genetics may dictate the predisposition to develop submental fat, lifestyle choices and targeted exercises can play a crucial role in managing its appearance, contributing to a more contoured and defined facial profile.

Spot Reduction: Challenges and Consistency

The concept of spot reduction—the idea that one can target fat loss in specific areas of the body—has long been a topic of debate among fitness and health professionals. When it comes to reducing a double chin, the challenge lies in the body's natural process of fat loss, which occurs uniformly rather than in isolated spots. This universal approach to shedding fat means that focusing solely on facial exercises, while beneficial for toning and strengthening the muscles beneath, may not directly result in the loss of submental fat without a comprehensive strategy.

However, this does not render facial exercises ineffective for those aiming to reduce their double chin. Consistency in performing these exercises plays a pivotal role in achieving noticeable results. The key lies in the combination of overall body fat reduction, which can be influenced by factors such as diet, hydration, and general physical activity, with targeted facial workouts that enhance muscle tone and improve the appearance of the jawline and neck area.

Muscle activation through facial exercises contributes to a more defined facial structure by engaging and strengthening the platysma and masseter muscles, among others involved in the contouring of the jawline and neck. Over time, as these muscles become more pronounced, the skin appears tighter, and the silhouette of the face becomes more sculpted. This muscle engagement, when paired with a reduction in overall body fat, can lead to a decrease in the appearance of a double chin.

The importance of consistency cannot be overstated. Just as with any muscle-building or fat-loss regimen, the effects of facial exercises accumulate gradually. Immediate results should not be expected, and patience is crucial. Incorporating these exercises into a daily routine ensures that the muscles are being stimulated regularly, which is essential for maintaining muscle tone and encouraging the redistribution of fat from the submental area.

Moreover, consistency in healthy living choices amplifies the benefits of facial exercises. A balanced diet rich in nutrients supports skin elasticity and muscle health, while adequate hydration ensures that the body functions optimally, aiding in the detoxification process and potentially reducing water retention, which can affect the appearance of the face and neck.

In conclusion, while spot reduction of fat in the double chin through facial exercises alone presents challenges due to the body's uniform approach to fat loss, consistent application of these exercises, combined with a holistic approach to health and fitness, offers a viable pathway to achieving a more defined jawline. The journey to reducing a double chin and enhancing facial contours is a marathon, not a sprint, requiring dedication, patience, and a comprehensive lifestyle approach that includes targeted exercises, proper nutrition, and overall physical activity.

The Role of Muscle Activation in Reducing Double Chin Fat

Muscle activation plays a crucial role in the process of reducing double chin fat and achieving a more sculpted jawline. When specific muscles are engaged, they not only help to tone the area but also promote better circulation and fat metabolism. This chapter delves into the importance of targeting the platysma muscle, the submental area, and the jawline to effectively combat the appearance of a double chin.

The platysma muscle, which runs from the jawline down to the collarbone, is often overlooked in traditional fitness routines. However, by focusing on this muscle, you can create a firmer and more defined chin. Engaging the submental area, located directly under the chin, is equally important as it helps to lift and tighten the skin, reducing sagging and excess fat.

Incorporating exercises that activate these muscles into your daily routine can lead to noticeable improvements in your facial contour. The key is to perform these exercises with intention, ensuring that you are fully engaging the target muscles while keeping the rest of your face relaxed. This focused approach not only enhances the effectiveness of the workout but also minimizes the risk of strain in other areas, such as the neck and shoulders.

As you progress through your facial shaping journey, remember that consistency is vital. Regularly activating these muscles will contribute to long-term results, helping you achieve a more youthful and confident appearance. By understanding the role of muscle activation in reducing double chin fat, you can empower yourself to take control of your facial aesthetics and boost your overall confidence..

Commitment Beyond 30 Days

Commitment to any fitness or beauty regimen is the cornerstone of achieving and maintaining the desired results, and the journey toward reducing a double chin and sculpting a more defined facial profile is no exception. The initial 30 days of diligently following the facial exercises outlined in this program serve as a foundational period, during which you begin to engage and strengthen the muscles of the neck and lower face. However, the true transformation, both in appearance and in muscle functionality, unfolds over a longer period. This extended commitment is crucial for several reasons, each contributing to the lasting success of your efforts.

Firstly, muscle memory plays a significant role in the effectiveness of any exercise routine. Just as with body workouts, facial exercises rely on the principle of repetition to train the muscles to hold a more lifted and toned position naturally. Over time, these muscles develop the strength and endurance needed to support the skin more firmly, contributing to a reduction in the appearance of a double chin. The initial 30 days are just the beginning of this process. Beyond this period, continued exercise ensures that the muscles not only reach their optimal tone but also maintain it, preventing regression and the return of sagging or fullness under the chin.

Moreover, the skin itself, much like the muscles beneath, benefits from ongoing care and stimulation. The increased blood flow and circulation that result from regular facial exercises promote skin health, enhancing its elasticity and appearance. This is particularly important for individuals in the target age range of 30 to 50, during which the skin naturally begins to lose some of its youthful resilience. Consistent exercise beyond the 30-day mark supports the skin's regenerative processes, helping to slow the visible signs of aging and maintain a more youthful complexion.

Another aspect to consider is the role of habit formation in the success of any long-term goal. Establishing a routine that includes facial exercises as a regular part of your daily self-care regimen ensures that the practice becomes second nature, much like brushing your teeth or applying sunscreen. This habitual integration into your lifestyle makes it more likely that you will stick with the exercises long enough to see significant changes, and more importantly, to sustain those changes.

Furthermore, the journey toward reducing a double chin and enhancing facial contours is not solely about physical appearance. It is also about nurturing a deeper connection with oneself, fostering self-care, and building confidence. The discipline and self-commitment required to continue the exercises beyond the initial challenge period reinforce a positive mindset and a proactive approach to personal health and beauty. This mental and emotional engagement with the process adds a layer of motivation that transcends the physical benefits, encouraging a longer-term commitment.

Lastly, it's important to acknowledge that the body's response to exercise, including facial exercises, can vary widely among individuals. Factors such as genetics, overall health, and lifestyle choices all play a part in how quickly and noticeably results manifest. By extending the commitment beyond 30 days, you allow yourself the time needed to observe these changes, adjust the routine as necessary, and truly tailor the exercises to meet your specific goals and needs.

In essence, the decision to continue with facial exercises beyond the initial 30-day challenge is a commitment to oneself. It's an acknowledgment that lasting change takes time, patience, and perseverance. By embracing this journey as a long-term investment in your health, beauty, and well-being, you set the stage for sustainable results that not only enhance your appearance but also boost your confidence and quality of life.

Exercises Explained and Beneficial

Chin Lift

Purpose: Aims to strengthen and tone the muscles under the chin and along the jawline, reducing the appearance of a double chin for a more defined facial contour.

Target Area: Focuses on the platysma muscle and submental area beneath the chin.

Step-by-Step Instructions

Starting Position: Sit in an upright position with your back straight and shoulders down. Keep your mouth closed and relax your face.

Movement:

1. Slowly tilt your head back until you are looking at the ceiling.
2. Press your tongue firmly against the roof of your mouth.
3. Keeping your tongue in place, slowly lower your chin to your chest as far as possible without rounding your upper back.
4. You should feel a strong contraction in the front of your neck and under your chin.
5. Hold this position for 5 seconds before releasing and returning to the starting position.
6. Repeat this movement 10 times for one set.

Duration/ Repetitions: Hold each contraction for 5 seconds. Perform 10 repetitions per set, aiming for 2-3 sets.

Pro Tips

- Ensure you maintain a straight posture throughout the exercise to maximize the engagement of the neck muscles.
- If you experience any discomfort in your neck, reduce the range of motion until you build up more strength.

Common Mistakes to Avoid

- Avoid jerking or using momentum to tilt your head back; the movement should be slow and controlled.
- Do not hold your breath; breathe normally throughout the exercise to ensure proper muscle oxygenation.

Tongue Stretch

Purpose: To stretch and strengthen the muscles under the chin, reducing the appearance of a double chin and promoting a more defined jawline.

Target Area: Submental area (under the chin) and the platysma muscle.

Step-by-Step Instructions

Starting Position: Sit or stand with your back straight and shoulders relaxed. Look straight ahead with your face in a neutral position.

Movement:

1. Open your mouth wide.
2. Stick your tongue out as far as you can, trying to reach your chin with the tip of your tongue.
3. Hold this stretch for 10 seconds, feeling the tension under your chin and in your neck.
4. Slowly retract your tongue and close your mouth, returning to the starting position.
5. Repeat this movement 10 times for one set.

Duration/ Repetitions: Hold the stretch for 10 seconds. Perform 10 repetitions per set, aiming for 2-3 sets.

Pro Tips

- Focus on extending the tongue as far as possible to maximize the stretch under the chin.
- Keep the rest of your face relaxed to avoid creating tension or wrinkles in other areas.

Common Mistakes to Avoid

- Avoid straining your neck forward; the movement should be isolated to the tongue and the stretch should be felt under the chin.
- Do not hold your breath during the stretch; breathe normally to ensure proper muscle oxygenation.

Jaw Jut

Purpose: Strengthen the muscles beneath the chin and along the jawline to achieve a more defined and sculpted facial profile

Target Area: Platysma and mentalis muscles, addressing submental fat (double chin)

Step-by-Step Instructions

Starting Position: Sit or stand with your spine aligned and shoulders relaxed, ensuring good posture for effective muscle engagement

Movement:

1. Tilt your head back to look towards the ceiling, creating a stretch along the front of your neck
2. Extend your lower jaw forward, feeling a stretch under the chin and along the jawline
3. Hold this position for a count of five to ten seconds, focusing on the tension in the muscles beneath the chin
4. Keep the rest of your face relaxed to prevent unnecessary wrinkles
5. Relax your jaw and return your head to a neutral position

Duration/ Repetitions: Repeat the movement for a total of ten to fifteen repetitions, ensuring consistent and controlled motions throughout

Pro Tips

Incorporate th s exercise into your daily routine for optimal results, and consider pairing it with other facial exercises targeting different areas of the face and neck for a balanced approach

Common Mistakes to Avoid

Avoid tensing other facial muscles, which can lead to unwanted wrinkles; ensure your posture is correct to prevent strain.

Neck Resistance Push

Purpose: To strengthen the neck muscles, reduce the appearance of a double chin, and promote a more defined jawline.

Target Area: Platysma muscle, neck muscles, and jawline.

Step-by-Step Instructions

Starting Position: Sit in an upright position on a chair with your feet flat on the ground. Keep your back straight, shoulders down, and look forward.

Movement:

1. Place your hands on your forehead.
2. Gently push your head forward while using your hands to create resistance. Your head shouldn't actually move forward but you should feel the neck muscles engaging.
3. Hold this position and the tension for 5 to 10 seconds.
4. Relax and return to the starting position.
5. Now, place your hands on the back of your head.
6. Gently push your head backward against your hands to create resistance, again making sure your head doesn't move backward.
7. Hold this position and the tension for 5 to 10 seconds.
8. Return to the starting position to complete one repetition.

Duration/ Repetitions: Perform 3 sets of 5 repetitions, with each push-hold lasting for 5 to 10 seconds.

Pro Tips

- Ensure you maintain a straight posture throughout the exercise to maximize engagement of the neck muscles.
- Adjust the amount of pressure with your hands to increase or decrease resistance based on your comfort level.
- Focus on slow, controlled movements to prevent any strain on the neck.

Common Mistakes to Avoid

- Avoid using too much force when pushing against your hands, which could lead to neck strain.
- Do not let your head actually move forward or backward; the movement should be resisted by your hands to ensure the neck muscles are properly engaged.
- Keep your shoulders relaxed and stationary to avoid creating tension in the shoulder and upper back area.

Ceiling Pout

Purpose: To reduce the appearance of a double chin and enhance the definition of the jawline

Target Area: Muscles under the chin and along the jawline

Step-by-Step Instructions:

Starting Position: Sit or stand with your back straight, embodying confidence and readiness.

Movement:

1. Tilt your head back gently until you are comfortably looking at the ceiling
2. Push your lower jaw forward to feel a stretch under your chin and along your jawline
3. Hold this position and form an exaggerated pout with your lips
4. Maintain the pouted position while breathing comfortably

Duration/ Repetitions: Hold the pout for 10 to 20 seconds and repeat the exercise 10 to 15 times per session

Pro Tips

Ensure controlled breathing to aid muscle relaxation and increase oxygen flow to the facial muscles for better results.

Common Mistakes to Avoid

Avoid straining your neck or shoulders; keep your movements smooth and controlled.

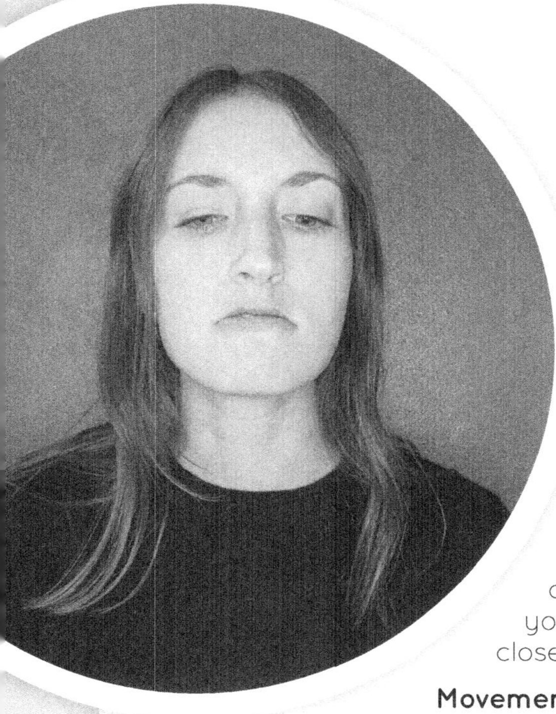

Jawline Sculptor

Purpose: To sculpt and define the jawline by strengthening the muscles around the jaw and chin, reducing the appearance of a double chin.

Target Area: Jawline, chin, and the muscles around the mouth.

Step-by-Step Instructions:

Starting Position: Sit in a comfortable chair with your back straight, shoulders relaxed, and head positioned directly over your shoulders. Keep your mouth closed and face relaxed.

Movement:

1. Begin by slightly opening your mouth.
2. With your mouth partially open, push your lower jaw out and lift your lower lip up as if you were trying to scoop water with it. You should feel a stretch build in your jawline and under your chin.
3. Hold this position for a count of 5-10 seconds, ensuring that you're engaging the muscles along your jawline and under your chin.
4. Relax your jaw and return to the starting position.
5. Repeat this movement 10 times for one set. Aim to complete 2-3 sets.

Duration/ Repetitions: Hold the position for 5-10 seconds. Perform 10 repetitions per set, completing 2-3 sets in total.

Pro Tips

- Ensure that you're only using the muscles of your lower face and jaw for this exercise. Keep the rest of your face as relaxed as possible to avoid creating tension or wrinkles.
- Breathe normally throughout the exercise to keep the muscles oxygenated.
- For added intensity, place a hand gently under your chin as resistance while pushing the jaw out.

Common Mistakes to Avoid

- Avoid tensing up your neck or shoulders. The movement should be isolated to the jaw and lower face.
- Do not clench your teeth together; keep them slightly apart to effectively engage the jawline muscles.
- Ensure not to overextend your jaw to the point of discomfort. The focus is on controlled, muscle-engaging movements.

Chin Tuck

Purpose: To strengthen the muscles of the neck and jawline, reducing the appearance of a double chin and promoting a more defined facial contour.

Target Area: Targets the platysma muscle and the area under the chin.

Step-by-Step Instructions

Starting Position: Sit or stand with your spine straight, shoulders rolled back and down, and look forward with your face in a neutral position.

Movement:

1. Gently lower your chin towards your chest, keeping your mouth closed and the back of your neck elongated.
2. Once you feel a stretch in the back of your neck, pause and hold this position.
3. Press your tongue against the roof of your mouth to engage the muscles under your chin further.
4. Hold this position for 5-10 seconds, focusing on the tension built in the neck and under the chin area.
5. Slowly lift your chin back to the starting position.
6. Repeat this movement 10 times for one set.

Duration/ Repetitions: Hold the tuck for 5-10 seconds. Perform 10 repetitions per set, aiming for 2-3 sets.

Pro Tips

- Ensure you maintain a gentle tension and do not overstretch, as the goal is to engage the muscles without straining.
- Keep the rest of your face relaxed to avoid creating tension in areas not targeted by this exercise.

Common Mistakes to Avoid

- Avoid pulling your chin too aggressively towards your chest, which can strain the neck.
- Do not hold your breath during the exercise; breathe normally to ensure proper oxygen flow to your muscles.

Troubleshooting Common Mistakes

One common mistake when engaging in facial exercises, particularly those aimed at reducing the double chin, is neglecting the importance of posture. Proper alignment of the spine and neck is crucial for effectively targeting the muscles under the chin and along the jawline. To correct this, always ensure your back is straight and your shoulders are drawn back and down. This alignment not only optimizes muscle engagement but also prevents strain and potential injury.

Another frequent oversight is the tendency to use too much force or to overextend the neck during exercises such as the Ceiling Pout. This can lead to neck strain and diminish the effectiveness of the exercise. Instead, focus on gentle, controlled movements. The goal is to feel a comfortable stretch and engagement of the muscles without causing discomfort. If you experience any pain, stop immediately and reassess your technique.

Breathing incorrectly is also a common pitfall. Many individuals hold their breath while performing facial exercises, which can lead to unnecessary tension in the face and neck. Remember, controlled breathing plays a significant role in the relaxation and proper engagement of muscles. Inhale deeply through the nose before beginning an exercise and exhale slowly through the mouth during the exertion phase of the exercise. This not only aids in muscle relaxation but also enhances oxygen flow to the facial muscles, promoting better results.

Skipping the warm-up is another mistake that can hinder the effectiveness of your facial workout routine. Just as with any physical exercise, warming up the facial muscles is essential for increasing blood circulation and preventing injury. Simple warm-up exercises such as gentle tapping, facial stretches, eye exercises, and neck rotations can significantly improve the flexibility and responsiveness of your facial muscles, making the subsequent exercises more effective.

Lastly, inconsistency and lack of patience are common challenges. Achieving noticeable results from facial exercises requires time and dedication. Many individuals become discouraged if they do not see immediate changes and may stop the exercises altogether. It's important to understand that like any form of physical fitness, changes in muscle tone and facial contouring take time. Consistency is key. Incorporate these exercises into your daily routine and give your muscles the time they need to strengthen and adapt. Celebrate small improvements and stay committed to your routine.

By addressing these common mistakes and implementing the recommended corrections, you can maximize the benefits of your facial exercises, reduce the appearance of a double chin, and enhance the overall definition of your jawline and facial contours. Remember, the journey to achieving a toned and sculpted face is a marathon, not a sprint. With patience, dedication, and proper technique, you can achieve the results you desire.

Avoid Jaw Tension and Wrinkles

Engaging the muscles of the jaw without creating tension or contributing to the formation of wrinkles requires a nuanced approach, blending mindfulness with precise physical action. The key lies in fostering an awareness of how much force is applied during exercises and ensuring that movements are smooth, controlled, and deliberate. Over-engagement or excessive force can not only strain the muscles but also lead to the development of fine lines and wrinkles, counteracting the rejuvenating effects of facial exercises.

To properly engage the jaw muscles without overdoing it, start by focusing on the sensation of the muscles being used. The goal is to activate them just enough to feel a gentle firming or tightening, without clenching or grinding the teeth. This can be achieved by maintaining a slight gap between the teeth during exercises, which naturally prevents excessive force. It's a simple yet effective way to ensure that the jaw muscles are engaged correctly without applying undue pressure or strain.

Another critical aspect is to incorporate relaxation techniques into the exercise routine. After completing a set of jaw exercises, take a moment to massage the muscles gently with your fingertips. This not only helps in relieving any tension that might have built up but also increases circulation to the area, aiding in the recovery and strengthening of the muscles. Additionally, practicing deep, controlled breathing throughout the exercises can further prevent the accumulation of tension, promoting a relaxed yet focused state that benefits both the mind and the facial muscles.

Visual cues can also play a significant role in ensuring proper engagement of the jaw muscles. Imagine a string gently lifting your jaw from the crown of your head, guiding the movement without forcing it. This visualization encourages a natural, tension-free engagement of the muscles, aligning with the principle of using the least amount of force necessary to achieve the desired effect. By visualizing the movement in this manner, you create a mental framework that supports the physical execution of the exercises, enhancing their effectiveness while minimizing the risk of creating wrinkles.

Moreover, consistency in practice is essential for mastering the technique of engaging the jaw muscles correctly. Regular, mindful practice allows you to develop a deeper understanding of your facial muscles and how they respond to different levels of engagement. Over time, this awareness will enable you to perform the exercises with greater precision, ensuring that you reap the maximum benefits without inadvertently contributing to wrinkle formation.

Incorporating these strategies into your facial exercise routine will not only help in reducing the appearance of a double chin and toning the jawline but also ensure that the skin remains smooth and free from the tension-induced wrinkles. By approaching the exercises with mindfulness, precision, and a focus on gentle engagement, you can achieve a sculpted, youthful appearance that reflects your commitment to natural beauty and self-care.

Chapter 4

Jawline Shaping

Jawline Anatomy and Muscle Tone

The jawline serves as one of the most defining features of the face, contributing significantly to one's facial silhouette and overall aesthetic appeal. A well-defined jawline is often associated with youthfulness and beauty, reflecting the underlying health and strength of facial muscles. The anatomy of the jawline is complex, involving a series of muscles, bones, and connective tissues that work in harmony to shape the lower contour of the face. Understanding this anatomy is crucial for anyone looking to enhance their facial definition through exercises and self-care practices.

At the core of the jawline's structure is the mandible, or lower jawbone, which is the largest and strongest bone in the face. It serves as the foundation upon which the muscles of mastication and facial expression attach. These muscles, including the masseter, temporalis, medial pterygoid, and lateral pterygoid muscles, play pivotal roles in chewing and speaking. However, their function extends beyond these basic movements, as they also contribute to the contour and firmness of the jawline.

The masseter, in particular, is key to the jawline's appearance. Located at the angle of the jaw, this muscle is one of the primary muscles used in chewing. When toned, the masseter muscle can help to create a more defined jawline by adding volume and shape to the sides of the face. Similarly, the platysma muscle, which spans the neck to the jaw, influences the appearance of the neck and the lower face. Toning this muscle through targeted exercises can reduce sagging and create a more youthful silhouette.

Muscle tone in the jawline area directly impacts its definition. When these muscles are strong and well-defined, they can significantly enhance the jawline's appearance, creating sharper angles and reducing the appearance of sagging or excess fat. Conversely, weak or underused muscles can lead to a softer, less defined jawline, contributing to a more aged appearance. This is why facial exercises that target these muscles can be so effective. By engaging and strengthening the muscles around the jawline, individuals can sculpt and tone this area, leading to improved facial contours and a more aesthetically pleasing profile.

Incorporating facial exercises into a daily routine can stimulate blood flow to the muscles and skin, promoting oxygenation and nutrient delivery, which are essential for maintaining muscle health and skin elasticity. Exercises such as jaw clenches, chin lifts, and neck stretches not only work the muscles but also encourage a tighter, more lifted appearance of the jawline and neck. Regular practice of these exercises can lead to noticeable improvements, with the jawline becoming more defined and the overall facial structure appearing more sculpted.

Moreover, understanding the role of posture and alignment in shaping the jawline is equally important. Proper alignment of the head, neck, and shoulders can enhance muscle function and appearance. A forward head posture or slouching can weaken the neck and jawline muscles over time, exacerbating the appearance of sagging and diminishing the definition of the jawline. Maintaining a neutral spine and practicing exercises that encourage proper posture can therefore complement facial exercises in achieving a more defined jawline.

In essence, the anatomy of the jawline and its surrounding muscles plays a crucial role in facial aesthetics. Strengthening these muscles through targeted exercises and maintaining good posture can significantly impact the jawline's definition, contributing to a more youthful and confident appearance. As individuals embark on this journey of facial sculpting, patience and consistency are key. With dedication to regular practice, the transformation of the jawline from soft and undefined to sharp and sculpted is not only possible but achievable, offering a natural and non-invasive path to enhancing one's beauty and self-esteem.

Cheek and Jaw Muscles for Sculpted Look

The cheek and jaw muscles are pivotal in defining the aesthetic contour of the face, playing a significant role in sculpting a look that exudes youthfulness and vitality. These muscles, when properly toned, contribute to the overall facial structure by providing the necessary support to the skin, thereby enhancing facial definition and reducing signs of aging such as sagging and jowls. The zygomaticus major and minor muscles, responsible for pulling the corners of the mouth upwards and backwards, and the masseter muscle, one of the strongest muscles in the body used for chewing, are particularly crucial in this regard. Strengthening these muscles through targeted exercises can lead to a more defined cheekbone area and a sharper jawline, features often associated with beauty and health.

For individuals aiming to achieve a sculpted look without resorting to invasive procedures, focusing on exercises that engage and tone these muscles can be remarkably effective. For instance, performing the "Cheek Sculptor" exercise, which involves inflating the cheeks with air and transferring the air from one cheek to the other, can significantly enhance cheek muscle tone. Similarly, the "Jaw Clenches" exercise, which targets the masseter muscle by clenching the jaw tightly and holding the position, can help in defining the jawline. These exercises not only work on the muscles but also improve blood circulation to the facial skin, promoting a healthy glow and aiding in the delivery of nutrients essential for muscle repair and growth.

Moreover, the role of these muscles extends beyond mere aesthetics. The cheek and jaw muscles are integral to facial expressions and communication. A well-toned musculature supports a wider range of expressions, contributing to more vibrant and dynamic interactions. This aspect underscores the importance of maintaining the health and strength of these muscles not just for their cosmetic benefits but also for their contribution to overall facial functionality.

Incorporating facial exercises into a daily self-care routine can be a game-changer for those seeking natural ways to maintain a youthful appearance. It's important to approach these exercises with patience and consistency, as the muscles of the face, like those in the rest of the body, require time to tone and strengthen. Additionally, combining facial exercises with a balanced diet rich in vitamins and minerals will support muscle health and skin elasticity, further enhancing the sculpted look.

The beauty of focusing on the cheek and jaw muscles lies in the simplicity and accessibility of the exercises designed to tone them. These exercises can be performed anywhere and at any time, making them a convenient option for busy individuals. Moreover, they offer a non-invasive alternative to cosmetic procedures, aligning with the growing preference for natural beauty solutions.

As we delve deeper into the intricacies of facial anatomy, it becomes evident that the cheek and jaw muscles are foundational to achieving a sculpted, defined look. Engaging in regular, targeted exercises that focus on these muscles can transform the face, highlighting its natural contours and enhancing its overall appearance. This approach not only promises aesthetic benefits but also fosters a deeper connection with one's body, encouraging a holistic view of health and beauty that transcends superficial enhancements. Through dedication to facial exercises, individuals can unlock the potential for a naturally sculpted appearance that radiates confidence and vitality.

Jawline Sculpting for Youthful Appearance

A strong, sculpted jawline is more than just a symbol of beauty; it's a hallmark of youth and vitality. As we age, the definition in our jawline can diminish due to a variety of factors including loss of muscle tone, accumulation of fat, and the natural decrease in skin elasticity. This can lead to a softer, less defined facial silhouette which many associate with aging. However, the good news is that through targeted jawline sculpting exercises, it's possible to counteract these effects, enhancing the jawline's definition and contributing to a more youthful appearance.

The jawline is framed by several key muscles, including the masseter, the strongest muscle in the face, which plays a crucial role in chewing. When these muscles are toned and strengthened through specific exercises, they can help to lift and define the lower face, creating a sharper, more defined jawline. This not only improves the overall facial structure but also helps to reduce the appearance of sagging skin and excess fat around the neck and chin area, common concerns that increase with age.

Moreover, a well-defined jawline affects how light and shadows play across the face, which can significantly impact perceived age. Sharp angles and defined contours are often associated with youthfulness, whereas softer, rounded edges can make the face appear older. By engaging in jawline sculpting exercises, you're essentially enhancing these natural shadows and highlights, giving your face a more youthful and dynamic appearance.

Incorporating jawline exercises into your daily routine doesn't require a significant time investment but can yield noticeable results. Simple yet effective exercises such as chin lifts, neck stretches, and jaw clenches can be performed almost anywhere, fitting easily into even the busiest of schedules. These exercises not only work towards sculpting the jawline but also promote better posture and breathing, which are essential for optimal muscle function and appearance.

The beauty of jawline sculpting exercises lies in their simplicity and the fact that they can be done without any special equipment. They offer a natural, non-invasive approach to maintaining a youthful appearance, aligning with the desires of many to find holistic and sustainable beauty solutions. Regular practice can lead to significant improvements, not just in the jawline, but in the overall health and vitality of the facial muscles and skin.

It's important to approach jawline sculpting with patience and consistency. Just like any other form of exercise, results won't appear overnight but developing a routine and sticking to it can lead to gradual and sustainable improvements. As the muscles become stronger and more defined, you'll likely notice not just a more sculpted jawline but also an increase in confidence and self-esteem, knowing that you're taking proactive steps to maintain your natural beauty and youthfulness.

Furthermore, complementing your exercise routine with a balanced diet rich in vitamins and minerals can enhance skin elasticity and muscle health, amplifying the effects of your efforts. Hydration also plays a critical role in maintaining skin plumpness and aiding in the detoxification process, which can further contribute to a more youthful appearance.

In essence, jawline sculpting is a powerful tool in the arsenal of natural beauty and anti-aging techniques. By dedicating a few minutes each day to targeted exercises, you can enhance your jawline's definition, combat signs of aging, and embrace a more youthful and radiant appearance. This approach not only offers aesthetic benefits but also fosters a deeper connection with your body, encouraging a holistic view of health, beauty, and well-being.

Skin Tightening vs. Muscle Strengthening

Achieving a sculpted, youthful appearance goes beyond simply focusing on either skin tightening or muscle strengthening alone; it necessitates a harmonious approach that addresses both aspects to yield optimal results. The skin and muscles of the face are intrinsically linked, with the condition of one directly impacting the appearance of the other. For those in the 30 to 50 age range, particularly women who are proactive about their physical appearance and health, understanding this balance is crucial.

Skin tightening is essential because, as we age, our skin loses elasticity due to decreased collagen and elastin production, leading to sagging and the formation of wrinkles. This natural process can be counteracted through targeted facial exercises that promote blood circulation, enhancing the delivery of oxygen and nutrients that support skin health. Additionally, incorporating skincare routines that include hydration, the use of retinoids, antioxidants, and peptides can further support the skin's elasticity and firmness. These topical solutions work on the surface level to improve skin texture and tightness, making it a critical component of a comprehensive facial sculpting regimen.

On the other hand, muscle strengthening is equally important. The facial structure benefits from a strong musculature underneath, as toned muscles provide the necessary support to the skin, helping to maintain its youthful contour and preventing sagging. Exercises that target the jawline, cheeks, and neck are particularly beneficial as they engage and strengthen the muscles responsible for the definition and shape of the face. Stronger muscles not only contribute to a more defined appearance but also play a role in reducing the visibility of fat deposits under the skin, such as those contributing to a double chin.

The synergy between skin tightening and muscle strengthening is where the true transformation occurs. Engaging in a routine that combines facial exercises with a diligent skincare regimen amplifies the benefits, leading to a more pronounced and lasting youthful appearance. For instance, following a facial exercise session with a skincare routine that includes products designed to soothe, repair, and hydrate the skin can enhance the exercise's effectiveness. The increased blood flow from the exercises improves the skin's ability to absorb and benefit from the nutrients and active ingredients in skincare products.

Moreover, lifestyle factors such as diet, hydration, and sun protection play a significant role in this balance. A diet rich in antioxidants, healthy fats, and vitamins supports skin health from the inside out, while adequate hydration ensures that the skin remains plump and elastic. Sun protection, on the other hand, prevents damage that can lead to premature aging and loss of skin elasticity. These elements, combined with regular facial exercises and a targeted skincare routine, create a comprehensive approach to facial sculpting that addresses both skin tightening and muscle strengthening.

For the health-conscious, goal-oriented woman who values self-care and seeks to maintain a youthful appearance without invasive procedures, understanding and implementing this balanced approach can be empowering. It offers a natural, holistic path to achieving and maintaining a sculpted, radiant complexion that reflects her commitment to her health and appearance. By dedicating time to both muscle strengthening exercises and a nourishing skincare routine, complemented by healthy lifestyle choices, she can achieve the optimal results that enhance her natural beauty and boost her confidence.

Jawline Exercises in Daily Routines

Incorporating jawline exercises into daily activities is a seamless way to enhance your facial sculpting routine without carving out additional time from your already packed schedule. The key is to integrate these exercises into habits and tasks that are already part of your routine, ensuring consistency and maximizing the potential for noticeable results. For the busy, health-conscious woman, making the most of moments throughout the day can turn idle or routine activities into opportunities for self-improvement and care.

Starting with the morning routine, while brushing your teeth or showering, you can perform the "Jaw Clenches" exercise. Clench your jaw firmly for a few seconds and then release. This simple exercise can be repeated several times, helping to tone the masseter muscle, which is crucial for defining the jawline. The repetition during this twice-daily habit ensures you're engaging these muscles regularly, setting a tone of self-care from the start of your day.

During your commute or while sitting at your desk, take advantage of the time to practice the "Neck Stretch." Gently tilt your head back to look at the ceiling and then slowly bring your head forward, bringing your chin towards your chest. This exercise not only targets the neck and jawline but also offers a moment of relaxation and stress relief, which is especially beneficial during a busy workday.

Lunch breaks offer another perfect opportunity. While seated, engage in the "Chin Lifts" by extending your lower jaw forward and then lifting your lower lip up as if trying to touch your nose with it. This can be done discreetly and requires only a few seconds per repetition, making it an ideal exercise to incorporate into short breaks throughout the day.

For those who enjoy an afternoon walk or a quick gym session, integrating the "Tongue Stretch" can enhance your jawline workout. Push your tongue against the roof of your mouth and then smile widely while keeping the tongue in place. This exercise engages the muscles underneath the chin and along the jawline, and doing this while walking or warming up for your workout adds no extra time to your routine.

Evening routines are also ripe with opportunities for jawline exercises. While preparing dinner or doing chores, you can perform the "Jaw Jut." Tilt your head back, look at the ceiling, and move your lower jaw forward, feeling a stretch under your chin. This exercise can be easily integrated into moments of waiting, such as while the water boils or the microwave counts down, turning these brief pauses into productive self-care moments.

Lastly, as you unwind in the evening, perhaps while reading or watching TV, take the time to practice the "Ceiling Pout." Tilt your head back, pout your lips as if aiming for the ceiling, and hold the position. This not only works the muscles but also serves as a relaxing end to your day, blending self-care with relaxation seamlessly.

By weaving these jawline exercises into your daily activities, you transform routine moments into opportunities for enhancing your facial definition and contributing to your overall sense of well-being. This approach ensures that even the busiest of schedules can accommodate effective jawline sculpting, proving that self-care and beauty routines do not have to be time-consuming to be effective. With creativity and commitment, every woman can integrate these exercises into her life, promoting not only a more defined jawline but also a lifestyle that prioritizes health, beauty, and self-confidence.

Exercises: Explanations and Benefits

Cheek Lift

Purpose: To lift and tone the cheeks, reducing sagging and enhancing facial contours for a more youthful appearance.

Target Area: Targets the zygomaticus major and minor muscles responsible for lifting the corners of the mouth and the buccinator muscles involved in cheek compression.

Step-by-Step Instructions

Starting Position: Sit or stand with your back straight, shoulders relaxed, and maintain a neutral head position. Breathe normally and keep your face relaxed.

Movement:

1. Open your mouth slightly and pull your lips inward over your teeth, creating a tight 'O' shape with your mouth.
2. Smile as wide as you can while keeping your lips over your teeth. You should feel a strong engagement in your cheek muscles.
3. Place your fingertips lightly on the top part of your cheeks, just below your eyes. This is not to apply pressure but to feel the muscles contracting.
4. Hold the smile position for 5 seconds, focusing on the lift in your cheeks.

5. Relax your smile slowly, returning to the starting position with your mouth slightly open and lips over your teeth.
6. Repeat this movement 10 times for one set.

Duration/ Repetitions: Hold each smile for 5 seconds. Perform 10 repetitions per set, aiming for 2-3 sets.

Pro Tips

- Ensure you're only using your cheek muscles to create the smile and lift, not your hands. Your fingertips are there solely for sensory feedback.
- Focus on smooth transitions between smiling and relaxing to maximize muscle engagement and control.
- Breathe evenly throughout the exercise to avoid holding your breath, which can create unnecessary tension in the face.

Common Mistakes to Avoid

- Avoid scrunching your eyes or forehead. The movement should be isolated to the cheeks and mouth area to prevent creating wrinkles in other areas of the face.
- Do not apply pressure with your fingers; they are there to guide and feel the muscles working, not to assist in the lift.
- Ensure not to overstretch the mouth or hold the smile too tightly, which can lead to muscle fatigue or strain.

Fish Face

Purpose: To sculpt a more defined jawline and enhance facial contours through targeted muscle engagement

Target Area: Muscles around the lips, cheeks, and jaw

Step-by-Step Instructions

Starting Position: Sit or stand comfortably with your back straight and shoulders relaxed.

Movement:

1. Draw your cheeks inward towards your teeth
2. Pucker your lips out as if preparing to kiss
3. Hold this position, feeling the stretch and contraction in your cheek muscles

Duration/ Repetitions: Hold for about five to ten seconds and repeat ten to fifteen times per session

Pro Tips

Focus on engaging the targeted muscles with each repetition, ensuring that you maintain proper posture throughout the exercise

Common Mistakes to Avoid

Avoid holding your breath while performing the exercise and ensure that your shoulders do not tense up.

The V Shape

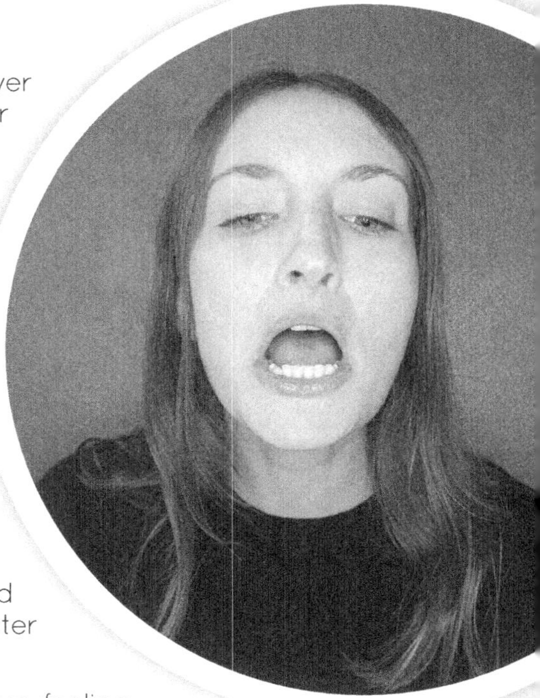

Purpose: To sculpt and define the lower half of your face, creating a sharper jawline and reducing sagging skin.

Target Area: Masseter muscles along the jaw and mentalis muscle at the chin.

Step-by-Step Instructions

Starting Position: Sit or stand with your spine straight, embodying confidence

Movement:

1. Open your mouth wide to stretch the jaw muscles, then contract the jaw muscles by pushing your lower jaw forward and upward as if scooping water with it.
2. Hold this position for a count of five, feeling the tension build in your jawline and under your chin.
3. Slowly return to the starting position.

Duration/Repetitions: Repeat the exercise ten times.

Pro Tips

For an intensified workout, add slight resistance by placing your hand against your chin while pushing forward to further engage the muscles.

Common Mistakes to Avoid

Avoid slouching or tensing other areas of your body; focus solely on the jaw and chin muscles to maximize effectiveness.

Jaw Push-Ups

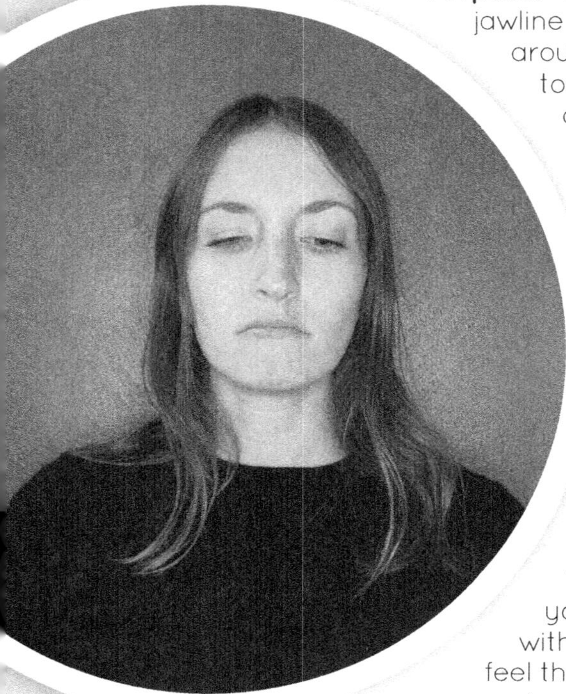

Purpose: To enhance the definition of the jawline and strengthen the muscles around the jaw and chin, contributing to a more sculpted facial appearance.

Target Area: Masseter muscle, jawline, and chin.

Step-by-Step Instructions

Starting Position: Sit in a comfortable position with your back straight and shoulders relaxed. Close your mouth gently with teeth slightly apart, ensuring your face and jaw are relaxed.

Movement:

1. Clench your jaw by pressing your teeth together firmly but without causing discomfort. You should feel the muscles on the sides of your jaw engaging.
2. While keeping your teeth pressed together, attempt to push your jaw forward as if trying to jut out your lower jaw beyond the upper jaw.
3. Hold this forward push for 3-5 seconds, focusing on the tension built along the sides of your jaw and under your chin.
4. Relax your jaw and return to the starting position with teeth slightly apart and jaw relaxed.
5. Repeat this forward push and hold for 10 repetitions to complete one set.

Duration/ Repetitions: Hold each push for 3-5 seconds. Perform 10 repetitions per set, aiming for 2-3 sets.

Pro Tips

- Ensure that the force used to clench the jaw is strong enough to engage the muscles but not so strong as to cause discomfort to the teeth or temporomandibular joint (TMJ).
- Focus on moving the jaw directly forward rather than upwards or downwards to specifically target the jawline muscles.
- Keep the rest of your face, especially your forehead and eyes, relaxed to avoid creating tension or wrinkles in other areas.

Common Mistakes to Avoid

- Avoid over-clenching your teeth or using excessive force, which can lead to jaw pain or TMJ issues.
- Do not hold your breath during the exercise; maintain normal breathing to ensure muscle oxygenation.
- Ensure not to strain your neck or shoulders during the movement; the motion should be isolated to the jaw.

Cheek Sculptor

Purpose: To enhance cheek definition and firmness by targeting and strengthening the cheek muscles, promoting a more youthful and sculpted facial appearance.

Target Area: Zygomaticus major and minor (cheek muscles).

Step-by-Step Instructions

Starting Position: Sit or stand with your spine in a neutral position, shoulders relaxed, and maintain a natural head posture. Ensure your face is relaxed and your jaw is slightly open.

Movement:

1. Expand your cheeks by filling them with air, similar to blowing up a balloon. Keep your lips sealed and your jaw slightly open.
2. Hold the air in your right cheek for 3 seconds, then transfer it to your left cheek, holding for another 3 seconds.
3. Continue to transfer the air back and forth between your cheeks for a total of 10 transfers.
4. After the final transfer, push all the air out of your mouth forcefully, engaging the muscles around your mouth and cheeks.
5. Repeat this entire sequence for 2-3 sets.

Duration/ Repetitions: 10 air transfers per set, with each hold lasting 3 seconds. Perform 2-3 sets.

Pro Tips

- Focus on using your cheek muscles to move the air rather than your tongue or mouth movements.
- Keep the rest of your face as relaxed as possible to isolate the cheek muscles and prevent creating tension or wrinkles in other areas.
- For an added challenge, try increasing the duration of each air hold or adding more air transfers per set.

Common Mistakes to Avoid

- Avoid tensing up your neck, shoulders, or forehead. The exercise should isolate the cheek muscles.
- Do not rush the air transfers. Moving the air slowly ensures better engagement and strengthening of the cheek muscles.
- Ensure not to overinflate your cheeks to the point of discomfort, which can strain the muscles.

Smiling Push

Purpose: To enhance the definition and tone of the jawline while promoting a youthful and vibrant appearance.

Target Area: Muscles around the mouth and cheeks.

Step-by-Step Instructions

Starting Position: Adopt a relaxed posture with shoulders down and back, ensuring your spine is straight for proper breathing and muscle engagement.

Movement:

1. Begin with a wide smile, stretching the corners of your mouth towards your ears as far as possible without discomfort.
2. While maintaining this smile, use your fingertips to gently push against the corners of your lips, creating slight resistance.
3. Hold this position for about five to ten seconds before relaxing.

Duration/ Repetitions: Repeat the exercise ten to fifteen times for optimal results.

Pro Tips

Focus on engaging the facial muscles fully during the push and maintain a relaxed demeanor to enhance the effectiveness of the exercise

Common Mistakes to Avoid

Avoid tensing your shoulders or neck during the exercise, as this can detract from the benefits and lead to discomfort.

Jaw Clenches

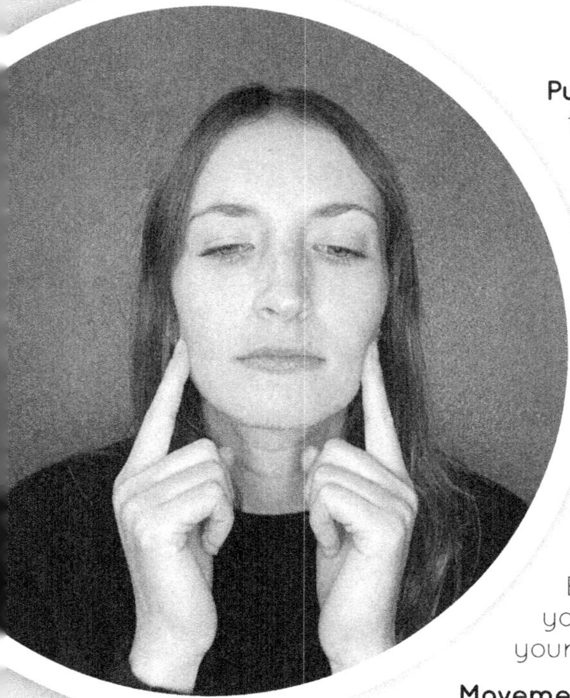

Purpose: To strengthen and define the jawline by engaging and toning the masseter muscle, which can help in reducing the appearance of a double chin and giving a more sculpted facial profile.

Target Area: Masseter muscle, jawline.

Step-by-Step Instructions

Starting Position: Sit or stand with your spine straight, shoulders down and relaxed. Keep your head in a neutral position, looking straight ahead. Ensure your mouth is closed and your teeth are slightly apart, relaxing your face and jaw.

Movement:

1. Gently clench your jaw by pressing your upper and lower teeth together. You should feel the muscles on either side of your jaw engage.
2. Increase the intensity of the clench gradually until you feel a strong but comfortable contraction in your jaw muscles.
3. Hold this clenched position for 5 seconds, focusing on the tension in the masseter muscles along the sides of your jaw.
4. Slowly release the clench, allowing your jaw muscles to relax completely before the next repetition.
5. Repeat the clench-and-hold movement for a total of 10 repetitions.

Duration/ Repetitions: Hold the clench for 5 seconds. Complete 10 repetitions per set, aiming for 2-3 sets.

Pro Tips

- To ensure maximum engagement of the jawline muscles, visualize trying to create a very slight smile as you clench, which can help activate more muscle fibers.
- Breathe normally throughout the exercise to avoid holding your breath, which can increase blood pressure unnecessarily.
- As you become more comfortable with the exercise, you can gradually increase the duration of each clench to 10 seconds for added intensity.

Common Mistakes to Avoid

- Avoid over-clenching to the point of discomfort, which can lead to jaw pain or temporomandibular joint (TMJ) issues.
- Ensure not to tense up your neck, shoulders, or other parts of your face during the exercise; the focus should be solely on the jaw muscles.
- Do not rush through the repetitions. The effectiveness of this exercise lies in the controlled, deliberate engagement and relaxation of the jaw muscles.

Wrinkle-Free Exercise Techniques

Performing facial exercises without creating wrinkles requires a nuanced approach that balances muscle engagement with skin care, ensuring that while we aim for a toned and sculpted jawline, we also preserve the skin's elasticity and smoothness. The key to achieving this balance lies in the mindfulness of movement, the precision of technique, and the integration of skin care practices that support the skin's health during your workout routine.

Firstly, focus on the quality of each movement rather than the quantity. Rushing through exercises or applying excessive force can not only strain muscles but also unnecessarily stretch the skin, contributing to wrinkle formation. Instead, execute each movement with control and awareness, paying close attention to the muscles you are engaging. This deliberate practice helps in isolating the target muscles effectively, reducing the need for overcompensation by surrounding areas and minimizing the risk of creating fine lines.

Secondly, maintain a relaxed face as much as possible during exercises. It's common to inadvertently tense other parts of the face, like the forehead or the area around the eyes, which can lead to wrinkles over time. To prevent this, regularly check in with yourself during exercises to ensure that you're not frowning, squinting, or puckering areas not involved in the current exercise. A helpful technique is to perform exercises in front of a mirror, allowing you to monitor your facial expressions and adjust as needed to keep the skin smooth and relaxed.

Incorporating a gentle touch supports the wrinkle-free approach. When exercises require applying pressure with your fingers, do so with a light, supportive touch. Avoid pulling or dragging the skin, which can contribute to loss of elasticity and formation of wrinkles. Use your fingers to guide rather than force movements, ensuring that your skin is treated with care and respect.

Hydration plays a crucial role in maintaining skin elasticity and preventing wrinkles. Ensure you are well-hydrated before starting your facial exercise routine, and consider applying a hydrating serum or moisturizer to help the skin remain supple. Well-hydrated skin can better withstand the movements of exercise without forming creases. Additionally, finishing your routine with a gentle massage using a moisturizer or facial oil can help soothe the skin, boost circulation, and encourage relaxation of the muscles, further contributing to a smooth, radiant complexion.

Lastly, integrate relaxation and stretching exercises for the face at the end of your routine. Just as with any other form of physical exercise, cooling down is essential. Gentle stretching can help release tension, promote muscle recovery, and prevent the formation of wrinkles. Techniques such as light tapping or soft patting over exercised areas encourage relaxation and can help in maintaining the skin's youthful appearance.

By adopting these techniques, you ensure that your journey to a more defined jawline and sculpted facial features is also a journey of caring for your skin's health and vitality. The goal is not only to enhance muscle tone but to nurture the skin, allowing your natural beauty to shine through without the concern of adding wrinkles to your canvas. Through mindful practice, precision, and a gentle approach, achieving a toned, youthful appearance while keeping your skin smooth and radiant is within reach.

Common Mistakes and Fixes

One of the most prevalent mistakes when engaging in jawline exercises is the incorrect alignment of the head and neck, which can not only diminish the effectiveness of the workout but also lead to strain and discomfort. To avoid this, ensure your head is positioned directly over your spine, not jutting forward or tucked into your chest. This alignment allows for maximum engagement of the jawline muscles without putting undue stress on the neck.

Another common error is overexertion. In the zeal to achieve quick results, there's a tendency to apply excessive force during exercises or to increase the number of repetitions beyond what is recommended. This overzealous approach can lead to muscle fatigue, soreness, and even injury. Remember, the goal of these exercises is to stimulate, not exhaust, the muscles. Focus on performing each exercise with precision and control, adhering to the recommended repetitions and intensity levels.

Breathing incorrectly or holding one's breath while performing facial exercises is another mistake that can hinder the effectiveness of your routine. Proper breathing ensures that the muscles receive the oxygen they need to function optimally and facilitates better muscle engagement. Make a conscious effort to breathe evenly and deeply through each exercise, inhaling and exhaling at a steady pace.

Neglecting the rest of the face and focusing solely on the jawline is a mistake that can lead to imbalanced results. While the jawline might be your primary area of concern, it's important to remember that the face works as a cohesive unit. Ignoring other facial muscles can result in disproportionate toning and definition. Incorporate exercises that target the cheeks, forehead, and neck to ensure a harmonious facial appearance.

Skipping the warm-up is a mistake that's easy to make, especially when pressed for time. However, warming up the facial muscles is crucial for preventing injury and enhancing the effectiveness of your exercises. A simple warm-up routine can include gentle tapping, facial stretches, or even a brief massage to increase circulation and prepare the muscles for the workout ahead.

Lastly, inconsistency is a common pitfall. Achieving and maintaining results requires regular practice and dedication. Skipping exercises or only doing them sporadically will not yield the desired outcomes. Set a realistic schedule for your facial exercise routine and stick to it, making adjustments as needed to accommodate your lifestyle and commitments.

By being mindful of these common mistakes and taking steps to avoid them, you can enhance the effectiveness of your jawline exercises, achieve better results, and ensure a safer, more enjoyable workout experience. Remember, the key to success lies in consistency, precision, and a holistic approach to facial fitness.

Chapter 5

Full-Face Toning Routine

Full-Face Toning for Balanced Results

Focusing on full-face toning is crucial for achieving balanced, symmetrical results that enhance the natural beauty of the entire face. When we concentrate our efforts solely on specific areas, such as the jawline or the cheeks, we risk creating an imbalanced appearance where some facial features may appear more defined or toned than others. This can lead to a look that feels disjointed rather than harmonious. The face is a complex structure of interconnected muscles, and when we engage in exercises that target the entire face, we ensure that all these muscles are strengthened and toned evenly. This holistic approach not only contributes to a more aesthetically pleasing outcome but also promotes overall facial health.

Moreover, full-face toning exercises contribute to improved skin elasticity and circulation, benefits that extend beyond muscle tone to affect the skin's appearance and health. By engaging in a comprehensive facial workout, we stimulate blood flow throughout the entire face, which can help to nourish skin cells and promote a radiant, youthful complexion. This increased circulation also aids in the efficient removal of toxins and can reduce the appearance of puffiness, further contributing to a more refreshed and vibrant look.

Another key aspect of full-face toning is its role in preventing and reducing the appearance of fine lines and wrinkles. As we age, our skin loses elasticity, and the muscles of the face can begin to weaken, leading to sagging and the formation of wrinkles. By incorporating exercises that target the entire face, we can help to counteract these effects, supporting muscle strength and skin tightness across the whole facial structure. This not only helps in maintaining a youthful appearance but also ensures that the face ages more uniformly, preserving natural symmetry and proportions.

Engaging in a full-face toning routine also offers practical benefits for those with busy lifestyles. By focusing on exercises that encompass the entire face, individuals can maximize their time and effort, achieving comprehensive results without needing to dedicate excessive time to their facial fitness regimen. This efficiency makes it easier to incorporate facial exercises into daily routines, ensuring consistency and facilitating long-term commitment to facial health and aesthetics.

In addition to the physical benefits, full-face toning exercises can also have a positive impact on mental well-being. The act of taking time to focus on oneself, to engage in self-care through facial exercises, can be a meditative and restorative practice. It offers an opportunity to connect with the body, to practice mindfulness, and to cultivate a sense of balance and well-being that radiates from the inside out.

Ultimately, the importance of full-face toning lies in its ability to produce balanced, comprehensive results that enhance the overall appearance and health of the face. By ensuring that all areas of the face are engaged and toned, we can achieve a harmonious, youthful look that reflects our commitment to holistic self-care. This approach not only benefits our physical appearance but also supports our overall health and well-being, underscoring the interconnectedness of facial fitness with the broader goals of health, beauty, and self-confidence.

Facial Muscle Interdependence

The human face is a marvel of biological engineering, with over fifty different muscles intricately woven together, each playing a pivotal role in facial expression, movement, and aesthetics. This complex network of muscles works in harmony, allowing for a vast array of expressions and contributing significantly to our non-verbal communication. Recognizing the interdependence of these muscles is crucial when embarking on a journey to enhance facial tone and aesthetics through exercise. Just as a well-orchestrated symphony relies on the contribution of each instrument to create a harmonious sound, the beauty and functionality of our face depend on the balanced interaction of all facial muscles.

When we smile, frown, or express surprise, we are not engaging a single muscle in isolation but rather a coordinated group of muscles. This interplay is what makes our expressions so rich and varied. For instance, the act of smiling involves not just the muscles around the mouth but also those around the eyes, cheeks, and even the neck. Similarly, a frown engages muscles in the forehead, eyes, and mouth. This interconnectedness means that when targeting facial fitness, focusing on isolated exercises for specific areas like the jawline or cheeks without considering the rest of the face can lead to imbalanced results. It's akin to training only one arm or leg; the asymmetry becomes noticeable and detracts from overall aesthetics.

To achieve balanced, symmetrical results, it's essential to engage in a full-face toning routine that considers the interplay between different muscle groups. This approach ensures that as some muscles are strengthened, their counterparts are also engaged, maintaining the natural balance and proportion of the face. For example, exercises that target the jawline should be complemented with exercises for the cheeks and neck to prevent an overly defined jawline that might appear disproportionate in relation to softer cheek muscles. Similarly, focusing on the forehead and eyes without addressing the lower face can result in an imbalanced appearance.

Moreover, the interconnectedness of facial muscles means that strengthening one area can have positive effects on adjacent areas. Strengthening the muscles around the mouth, for instance, can also lead to a reduction in nasolabial folds and marionette lines, as well as a more defined jawline, as these areas are supported by the same underlying muscular structure. This holistic approach not only enhances the overall appearance but also promotes a more youthful look, as a well-toned face tends to exhibit fewer signs of aging.

Incorporating a variety of exercises that target all areas of the face is therefore not just about aesthetics but also about achieving a balanced and healthy facial structure. Exercises that promote flexibility and strength across the face can improve blood circulation, skin elasticity, and even alleviate tension headaches and jaw pain caused by stress or TMJ disorders. The key is consistency and a well-rounded routine that acknowledges the symbiotic relationship between different facial muscles.

As we engage in this holistic approach to facial fitness, it's also important to remember that the benefits extend beyond the mirror. The act of performing facial exercises can be a form of self-care, offering a moment of mindfulness and relaxation in our busy lives. By focusing on the movement and engagement of our facial muscles, we can foster a deeper connection with our body, enhancing not just our physical appearance but also our overall well-being.

In essence, understanding and respecting the interdependence of facial muscles lays the foundation for a successful facial fitness regimen. It encourages a comprehensive approach that yields balanced, harmonious results, reflecting the intricate symphony of movements and expressions that make each face uniquely beautiful.

Targeting Multiple Zones for Symmetry

Targeting multiple zones at once during your facial exercise routine is a strategic approach that ensures balanced and symmetrical results, enhancing the natural beauty and harmony of your facial features. This method acknowledges the interconnectedness of facial muscles and the importance of a comprehensive workout that addresses the entire face rather than isolating specific areas. By engaging various muscle groups simultaneously, you not only streamline your workout regimen but also promote uniform muscle tone and skin elasticity across the face, which is essential for achieving a youthful and vibrant appearance.

The face is a complex structure where muscles are intricately linked, often supporting and counterbalancing each other. For instance, the muscles around the eyes and forehead are connected to those around the mouth and jawline. Therefore, focusing solely on the jawline without considering the forehead can lead to disproportionate muscle development, which might detract from the overall aesthetic appeal. By incorporating exercises that target the forehead, cheeks, jawline, and neck in a single routine, you ensure that each area receives attention, leading to a more balanced and cohesive facial structure.

Moreover, targeting multiple zones at once maximizes the efficiency of your facial fitness regimen. In today's fast-paced world, finding time for self-care can be challenging. A full-face toning routine that addresses multiple areas simultaneously fits perfectly into a busy schedule, allowing for significant results without requiring hours of commitment. This efficiency not only makes the routine more manageable but also increases the likelihood of consistency, which is key to seeing lasting changes.

Another advantage of this holistic approach is the enhanced circulation and skin rejuvenation that comes from a full-face workout. Stimulating blood flow to the entire face can improve nutrient delivery and toxin removal, which supports skin health and can lead to a more radiant complexion. This comprehensive stimulation is crucial for maintaining skin vitality and can help in reducing the signs of aging, such as fine lines and wrinkles, across the entire face.

Furthermore, engaging in a full-face toning routine can have psychological benefits, fostering a sense of achievement and well-being. Completing a comprehensive workout that leaves no area neglected can be incredibly satisfying, boosting confidence in your appearance and in your ability to take control of your aging process. This psychological boost is an important aspect of self-care, contributing to overall happiness and satisfaction with one's appearance.

Incorporating a variety of exercises that target different facial zones also allows for customization based on individual needs and goals. While the objective is to maintain balance, some areas may require more focus than others, depending on your unique facial structure and concerns. A routine that includes a wide range of exercises provides the flexibility to adjust focus as needed while still ensuring that the entire face benefits from a workout.

In practice, targeting multiple zones at once could involve combining exercises such as forehead smoothers, cheek lifts, and jawline sculpting movements in a single session. This not only ensures that each area is toned but also helps in maintaining the proportional relationships between different parts of the face, which is crucial for a harmonious appearance. As you progress with your routine, you may find that certain areas respond more quickly than others, allowing you to adjust the intensity and focus of your exercises to maintain balance and symmetry.

Ultimately, the goal of targeting multiple zones at once is to achieve a balanced, youthful, and radiant appearance that reflects your commitment to holistic facial health. By embracing a comprehensive approach to facial fitness, you can enjoy the benefits of a toned, sculpted face that exudes natural beauty and confidence.

Maintain Symmetry in Facial Workouts

Maintaining symmetry and avoiding the over-working of specific areas during your facial toning routine are crucial for achieving balanced and harmonious results. The key to this lies in a mindful approach to your exercises, ensuring that each part of your face receives equal attention and effort. To prevent the common pitfall of focusing too much on one area—often driven by a desire to correct a perceived flaw—it's important to develop a holistic view of facial fitness. Start by mapping out a routine that evenly targets all the major muscle groups in your face and neck. This includes the forehead, eyes, cheeks, jawline, and neck. By designing a balanced routine, you ensure that no single area is either neglected or over-emphasized.

One effective strategy is to rotate exercises daily or weekly, which not only prevents boredom but also ensures that all areas of the face are worked evenly over time. For instance, if your routine on Monday focuses more on the jawline and neck, make sure that Tuesday's routine shifts focus to the forehead and eyes. This rotation principle keeps the facial muscles guessing and avoids the plateau effect, where progress stalls due to the muscles becoming overly accustomed to a specific set of movements.

Another important aspect is to monitor the intensity and duration of exercises for each facial area. It's easy to overdo exercises for problem areas in hopes of quick results, but this can lead to muscle fatigue, strain, or even injury. Instead, practice each exercise with equal intensity and for an equal amount of time, ensuring that all facial muscles develop at a similar rate. Use a timer if necessary to keep your sessions balanced.

Symmetry in facial exercises also extends to the left and right sides of the face. Many individuals have a dominant side that they unconsciously favor, leading to uneven muscle development. To counteract this, perform an equal number of repetitions on each side, and periodically check in with a mirror to ensure that both sides are engaging equally. If you notice an imbalance, consciously focus on engaging the weaker side until symmetry is achieved.

Incorporating mindfulness into your routine can also enhance symmetry. Pay close attention to the sensations in your face as you exercise. This heightened awareness can help you detect imbalances in muscle engagement and effort. If one side of your face feels more strained or less engaged, adjust your technique accordingly. Mindfulness not only improves the effectiveness of your exercises but also turns your routine into a meditative practice, offering mental as well as physical benefits.

Finally, remember that rest is just as important as the exercises themselves. Overworking your facial muscles without adequate recovery can lead to tension, fatigue, and the potential for asymmetrical results. Ensure that you include rest days in your routine, allowing your muscles to recover and grow stronger. This balanced approach to facial fitness—combining thoughtful exercise selection, rotation, equal intensity, mindfulness, and rest—will help you achieve the symmetrical, toned, and youthful appearance you desire, without the risk of overworking specific areas.

Exercises and Benefits

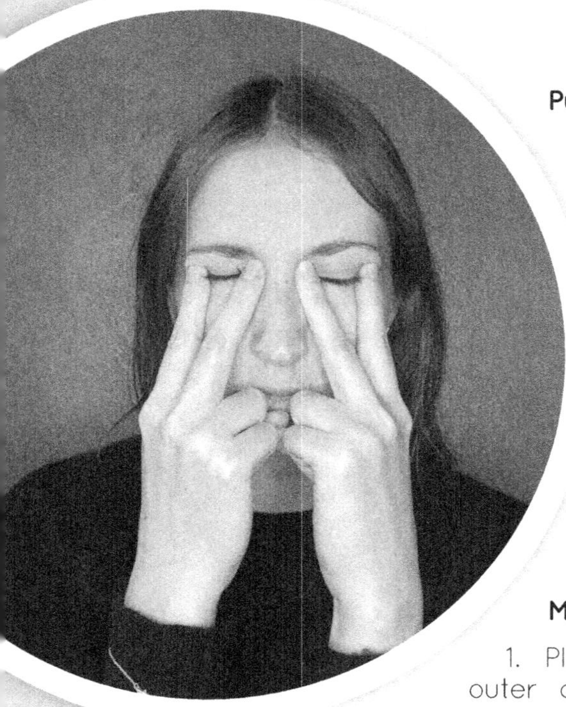

Eye Area Lift

Purpose: To reduce the appearance of fine lines and wrinkles around the eyes by strengthening and toning the orbicularis oculi muscle, promoting a more youthful and alert appearance.

Target Area: Orbicularis oculi muscle surrounding the eye.

Step-by-Step Instructions

Starting Position: Sit comfortably with your back straight and shoulders relaxed. Keep your face relaxed and maintain a neutral expression.

Movement:

1. Place your index fingers lightly at the outer corners of your eyes and your middle fingers at the inner corners of your eyes, just below the brow bone.
2. Apply gentle pressure with your fingertips, being careful not to tug or pull the skin.
3. While keeping your fingers in place, attempt to close your eyes tightly but without wrinkling your forehead. You should feel resistance from your fingers.
4. Hold the squeeze for 5 seconds, focusing on the contraction of the muscles around your eyes.
5. Slowly relax the squeeze and open your eyes, returning to the starting position.
6. Repeat this movement 10 times for one set.

Duration/ Repetitions: Hold each squeeze for 5 seconds. Perform 10 repetitions per set, aiming for 2-3 sets.

Pro Tips

- Ensure your forehead remains smooth throughout the exercise to isolate the work in the eye area and avoid creating forehead wrinkles.
- Breathe normally during the exercise to maintain relaxation in the rest of your face.
- As you become more comfortable with the exercise, focus on increasing the intensity of the squeeze for better muscle engagement.

Common Mistakes to Avoid

- Avoid pulling or stretching the skin around the eyes, as this can contribute to wrinkles rather than prevent them.
- Do not engage the forehead or brow muscles; the movement should be isolated to the eye area only.
- Ensure not to hold your breath during the exercise, as this can create unnecessary tension in the face.

Forehead Smoother

Purpose: To smooth out forehead lines and wrinkles by strengthening and toning the frontalis muscle, promoting a more relaxed and youthful forehead appearance.

Target Area: Frontalis muscle (forehead).

Step-by-Step Instructions

Starting Position: Sit or stand in a comfortable position with your back straight and shoulders relaxed. Keep your face relaxed and maintain a neutral expression.

Movement:

1. Place both hands on your forehead, fingers spread wide and palms gently resting against your skin.
2. Apply slight pressure with your fingertips and slowly slide your hands outward towards your temples, stretching the skin on your forehead.
3. While keeping the tension, try to raise your eyebrows as if surprised, against the resistance created by your hands. You should feel the frontalis muscle engaging under your fingertips.
4. Hold this raised eyebrow position for 5 seconds, focusing on the muscle contraction.
5. Relax your eyebrows and return to the starting position, removing your hands from your forehead.
6. Repeat this movement 10 times for one set.

Duration/ Repetitions: Hold each eyebrow raise for 5 seconds. Perform 10 repetitions per set, aiming for 2-3 sets.

Pro Tips

- Ensure your hands provide just enough resistance to feel the muscle work without causing skin stretching or pulling.
- Keep the rest of your face relaxed to focus the exercise solely on the forehead area.
- Breathe normally throughout the exercise to maintain relaxation and proper muscle engagement.

Common Mistakes to Avoid

- Avoid pulling or dragging the skin too hard with your hands, which could lead to wrinkles rather than prevent them.
- Do not tense up other parts of your face, such as squinting your eyes or puckering your lips, as this can counteract the benefits of the exercise.
- Ensure not to hold your breath during the exercise, as this can create unnecessary tension in the face and neck.

Crow's Feet Smoother

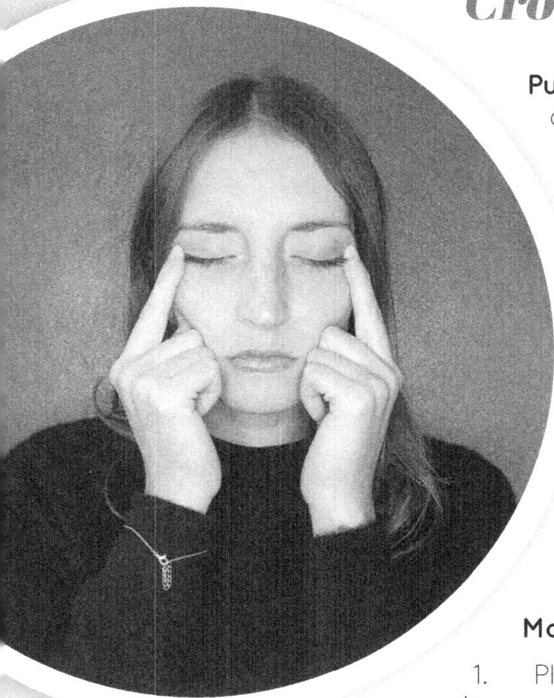

Purpose: To minimize the appearance of crow's feet by strengthening and toning the orbicularis oculi muscle, promoting smoother skin around the eyes.

Target Area: Orbicularis oculi muscle (around the eyes).

Step-by-Step Instructions

Starting Position: Sit or stand in a comfortable position with your back straight and shoulders relaxed. Keep your face relaxed and maintain a neutral expression.

Movement:

1. Place your index fingers lightly at the outer corners of your eyes.
2. Gently pull the skin towards your temples just until you feel a slight tension, not enough to tug or stretch the skin.
3. With your fingers still in place, attempt to close your eyes while keeping your forehead relaxed. You should feel a slight resistance against the closing motion.
4. Hold this position for 5 seconds, focusing on the engagement of the muscles around your eyes.
5. Slowly release and relax your eyes, returning to the starting position.
6. Repeat this movement 10 times for one set.

Duration/ Repetitions: Hold for 5 seconds. Perform 10 repetitions per set, aiming for 2-3 sets.

Pro Tips

- Ensure you're only applying enough tension to feel resistance without stretching the skin, as overstretching can contribute to wrinkles.
- Keep the rest of your face as relaxed as possible to isolate the exercise to the eye area.
- Breathe normally throughout the exercise to maintain overall facial relaxation.

Common Mistakes to Avoid

- Avoid pulling the skin too tightly, as this can cause more harm than good by potentially creating additional wrinkles.
- Do not engage your forehead or squint excessively; the goal is to work the muscles around the eyes specifically.
- Ensure not to skip the relaxation phase between repetitions, as this allows the muscles to recover and prevents overworking.

Smile Line Reducer

Purpose: To reduce the appearance of smile lines by toning and strengthening the muscles around the mouth and cheeks, promoting smoother skin.

Target Area: Orbicularis oris muscle (around the mouth) and zygomaticus major and minor (cheek muscles).

Step-by-Step Instructions

Starting Position: Sit or stand with your back straight and shoulders relaxed. Keep your face neutral without any tension.

Movement:

1. Begin by closing your mouth and pressing your lips together firmly but without straining.
2. Smile as wide as you can while keeping your lips pressed together; you should feel a stretch in your cheeks and around your mouth.
3. Place your fingers on the corners of your mouth and gently apply pressure to resist the smiling motion, creating tension.
4. Hold this position for 5-10 seconds, focusing on the muscles around the mouth and cheeks.
5. Relax your smile slowly, returning to the starting position.
6. Repeat the movement 10 times for one set.

Duration/Repetitions: Hold each smile for 5-10 seconds. Perform 10 repetitions per set, aiming for 2-3 sets.

Pro Tips

- Ensure you maintain a firm pressure with your lips throughout the exercise to fully engage the target muscles.
- Use only gentle pressure with your fingers to avoid stretching the skin; the focus is on creating muscle resistance.
- As you progress, try to increase the duration of each hold to intensify the exercise without compromising form.

Common Mistakes to Avoid

- Avoid overstretching the skin with your fingers; the resistance should come from the muscles, not skin tension.
- Do not hold your breath during the exercise; maintain steady, relaxed breathing to enhance muscle relaxation and engagement.
- Ensure not to tense up your neck or shoulders during the exercise; keep the focus on your face.

Forehead Tap

Purpose: To stimulate blood circulation and relax the muscles of the forehead, helping to reduce the appearance of horizontal forehead lines.

Target Area: Frontalis muscle (forehead).

Step-by-Step Instructions

Starting Position: Sit or stand comfortably with your shoulders relaxed and your face in a neutral, relaxed expression.

Movement:

1. Begin by warming your fingertips by rubbing them together until they feel warm.
2. Place the tips of your fingers on the center of your forehead.
3. Gently tap your forehead with your fingertips, moving outward towards your temples.
4. Continue this tapping motion for 30 seconds, covering the entire forehead area.
5. After completing the tapping motion, place your palms on the sides of your forehead, and gently sweep your hands outward towards your temples to finish the exercise.

Duration/ Repetitions: Perform the tapping motion for 30 seconds, followed by the sweeping motion once per set. Aim for 2-3 sets.

Pro Tips

- Ensure your hands are clean to avoid transferring oils or dirt to your face.
- Keep the tapping light and gentle to stimulate blood flow without causing redness or irritation.
- Focus on breathing deeply and evenly throughout the exercise to enhance relaxation and the benefits of the exercise.

Common Mistakes to Avoid

- Avoid tapping too hard, as this can lead to irritation or even bruising of the delicate skin on the forehead.
- Do not drag your fingers across your skin; the motion should be a light, lifting tap to avoid stretching the skin.
- Ensure not to focus solely on one area of the forehead; distribute the tapping evenly across the entire forehead to ensure all areas receive stimulation.

Under-Eye Lifter

Purpose: To strengthen and tone the muscles beneath the eyes, reducing the appearance of under-eye bags and promoting a more youthful and refreshed look.

Target Area: Orbicularis oculi muscle (around the eyes).

Step-by-Step Instructions

Starting Position: Sit or stand with your back straight and shoulders down, maintaining a relaxed posture. Keep your face relaxed without any tension.

Movement:

1. Place your index fingers lightly under each eye, following the natural curve of your lower eyelids.
2. Gently press upward and outward towards the temples, providing a slight resistance.
3. While keeping your fingers in place, attempt to close your eyes and squint slightly, feeling the resistance created by your fingers.
4. Hold this squinting position for 3-5 seconds, focusing on the contraction of the muscles beneath your eyes.
5. Slowly relax your squint, allowing your eyelids to return to their natural position, and remove your fingers.
6. Repeat this movement 10 times for one set.

Duration/Repetitions: Hold each squint for 3-5 seconds. Perform 10 repetitions per set, aiming for 2-3 sets.

Pro Tips

- Ensure that your fingers provide just enough resistance to feel the muscle work without causing any discomfort or pulling on the delicate skin around the eyes.
- Keep the rest of your face as relaxed as possible to isolate the exercise to the under-eye area.
- Breathe normally throughout the exercise to help maintain relaxation and proper muscle engagement.

Common Mistakes to Avoid

- Avoid pressing too hard or pulling the skin, as this can cause irritation or increase the risk of wrinkles.
- Do not tense up other facial muscles during the exercise; the focus should be solely on the muscles beneath the eyes.
- Ensure not to skip the relaxation phase between repetitions, as this allows the muscles to recover and prevents overworking.

Avoid Skin Overstretching and Wrinkling

To avoid overstretched skin and the formation of wrinkles while engaging in facial exercises, it's essential to adopt a gentle approach that respects the skin's natural elasticity and limits. The skin on our face, particularly around the eyes and mouth, is delicate and susceptible to damage if stretched excessively or improperly. One fundamental principle to adhere to is the concept of moderation. When performing any facial exercise, the movement should be smooth and controlled, never forcing the skin into unnatural or exaggerated positions. This ensures that while the underlying muscles are effectively engaged, the skin itself is not unduly strained.

Applying a light touch is another critical strategy. Instead of using heavy pressure or aggressive manipulation, use the fingertips to guide movements softly. This technique helps in targeting the muscles without putting unnecessary stress on the skin. For exercises that require direct skin contact, such as massages or stretches, ensure your hands are clean and possibly slightly moisturized to reduce friction and prevent dragging or pulling the skin.

Hydration plays a pivotal role in maintaining skin elasticity. Well-hydrated skin is more pliable and resilient, making it better equipped to handle the movements involved in facial exercises without succumbing to damage. Drinking plenty of water throughout the day and using a quality moisturizer suited to your skin type can significantly enhance the skin's natural barrier and elasticity. Before starting your facial exercise routine, applying a light, non-comedogenic moisturizer can also provide an additional layer of protection, helping the skin to glide more smoothly during exercises.

Understanding the limits of your own skin is crucial. Pay attention to how your skin feels during exercises; if you notice any discomfort or excessive pulling, adjust your technique accordingly. It's important to remember that the goal of these exercises is to promote a healthy, toned appearance, not to stretch the skin excessively. If an exercise feels too intense, reduce the range of motion or the number of repetitions to a level that feels comfortable.

Incorporating exercises that focus on building muscle tone rather than stretching the skin can also help minimize the risk of damage. Exercises designed to enhance muscle tone will naturally lift and firm the face without the need for excessive skin stretching. This approach not only helps in achieving a more youthful appearance but also ensures the integrity of the skin is maintained.

Finally, always conclude your facial exercise routine with gentle relaxation techniques. This can include light tapping or soft massages that help soothe the skin and muscles, promoting relaxation and recovery. These techniques aid in reducing any potential strain caused during the exercises and ensure that the skin remains supple and resilient.

By adhering to these guidelines, you can effectively engage in a full-face toning routine that enhances your appearance without compromising the health and integrity of your skin. The key is to exercise mindfulness and gentleness in every step of your routine, ensuring that your skin is treated with the care and respect it deserves.

Protecting Delicate Eye Areas

The delicate areas around the eyes demand special attention during facial exercises to prevent unnecessary strain or damage, which could lead to premature wrinkling or sagging. Given the thinness and sensitivity of the skin in this region, it's imperative to approach exercises targeting or involving the eye area with a gentle, mindful technique. This ensures that while the surrounding muscles are engaged and toned, the skin itself is preserved, maintaining its elasticity and vitality.

First and foremost, when engaging in exercises that impact the eye area, it's crucial to minimize any direct pressure on the eyelids or the skin directly under the eyes. Instead, focus on movements that encourage muscle engagement without stretching the skin excessively. For instance, exercises that involve squinting or opening the eyes wide should be performed with a soft intensity, ensuring that the skin is not being pulled too taut. This approach helps to activate the muscles without putting undue stress on the skin.

Another key strategy is to incorporate exercises that strengthen the muscles around the eyes indirectly. By focusing on the forehead or cheeks, for example, you can still stimulate muscle activity that supports the eye area without directly manipulating the delicate skin. This indirect method of toning can be particularly effective in maintaining the skin's integrity while still achieving the desired lift and firmness in the facial contours.

Hydration is also a critical factor in protecting the delicate eye areas during your facial exercise routine. Well-hydrated skin is more resilient and can better withstand the movements involved in facial exercises. Ensure you're drinking ample water throughout the day and consider using a hydrating eye cream or serum to provide additional moisture and nourishment to the eye area. Products containing hyaluronic acid, for example, can be especially beneficial in maintaining the skin's plumpness and elasticity.

Before and after performing your facial exercises, gently applying a cooling gel or mask around the eyes can also help soothe and protect the skin. This not only provides a refreshing sensation but can also reduce any potential inflammation or stress caused by the exercises. Look for products with calming ingredients like cucumber, aloe vera, or green tea, which offer natural anti-inflammatory benefits.

When performing any facial exercise routine, always listen to your body, especially when it comes to the delicate areas around your eyes. If you experience any discomfort or strain, modify the exercise to reduce intensity, or skip it altogether. Remember, the goal is to enhance your appearance and well-being, not to cause harm or discomfort.

Incorporating these protective measures into your facial exercise routine will ensure that the delicate areas around your eyes are preserved and cared for. By approaching these exercises with gentleness, mindfulness, and an emphasis on hydration and indirect muscle engagement, you can achieve a toned, youthful appearance while safeguarding the health and beauty of your skin.

Chapter 6

Neck and Chin Tightening Exercises

Neck and Chin Muscles for Facial Definition

The neck and chin muscles play a pivotal role in the overall aesthetics of the face, acting as the foundation upon which facial features are sculpted and defined. These muscles, when toned and strengthened, contribute significantly to the appearance of a youthful and lifted facial contour. The platysma, a broad sheet of muscle extending from the chest up to the jawline, and the digastric muscles, located under the jaw, are particularly influential in defining the neck and lower face. Their condition can dramatically affect the visual harmony and balance of the face.

A well-defined jawline and a tight, smooth neck are often seen as hallmarks of beauty and youth. However, as we age, these areas can become areas of concern due to skin laxity and the accumulation of submental fat, commonly referred to as a double chin. Engaging in targeted exercises that focus on these muscles can help counteract these signs of aging by building muscle tone and encouraging a firmer, more lifted appearance. This not only enhances the jawline but also reduces the appearance of a double chin, leading to a more refined and sculpted facial profile.

Strengthening the neck and chin muscles does more than just improve physical appearance; it also supports the skin's underlying structure. As these muscles become more robust, they can better support the skin, reducing sagging and contributing to a smoother, tighter skin texture. This muscular foundation is crucial for maintaining facial elasticity and combating the gravitational pull that leads to sagging over time.

Moreover, the engagement of these muscles through specific exercises encourages increased blood circulation to the face and neck. This enhanced circulation delivers oxygen and nutrients more efficiently, promoting skin health and vitality. The result is not only a more defined facial structure but also a complexion that appears brighter and more rejuvenated.

Incorporating exercises that target the neck and chin into a daily facial exercise routine offers a non-invasive solution to addressing concerns related to aging and skin laxity in these areas. These exercises are designed to be simple yet effective, allowing individuals to achieve noticeable results without the need for surgical interventions. Regular practice can lead to significant improvements in the appearance of the neck and chin, contributing to an overall more youthful and balanced facial aesthetic.

The connection between the neck and chin muscles and facial aesthetics is undeniable. By focusing on strengthening these key areas, individuals can enhance their natural beauty, boost their confidence, and enjoy a more youthful appearance. The benefits of such exercises extend beyond mere aesthetics, offering a holistic approach to facial health and well-being that supports both the physical and psychological aspects of beauty.

Strengthening the Neck for Facial Sculpting

Strengthening the neck is a critical component of any comprehensive facial sculpting routine, offering a multitude of benefits that extend beyond the immediate visual enhancements. The neck, often overlooked in favor of more prominent facial features, plays a foundational role in the overall appearance and structure of the face. By focusing on the neck muscles, individuals can achieve a more defined jawline, reduce the appearance of sagging skin, and enhance the contour of their facial profile. This approach not only leads to a more youthful and lifted appearance but also supports the structural integrity of the entire facial region.

The platysma, one of the key muscles in the neck, when toned, helps tighten the skin of the neck and lower jaw, acting as a natural lift for the face. This muscle, along with others in the neck, supports the facial tissues and can significantly impact the appearance of the face. Exercises targeting the platysma and surrounding neck muscles are essential for anyone looking to achieve a firmer, more sculpted look without resorting to invasive procedures.

One of the primary advantages of incorporating neck exercises into a facial sculpting routine is the promotion of better posture. A strong, toned neck naturally encourages the head to sit more squarely on the shoulders, reducing the forward tilt that often contributes to the formation of a double chin and sagging skin. Improved posture not only enhances the aesthetic appeal of the neck and jawline but also contributes to better alignment and function of the entire body.

Moreover, engaging the neck muscles through targeted exercises can increase blood flow to the face and neck area. This enhanced circulation delivers essential nutrients and oxygen to the skin, promoting cell renewal and improving skin health. The result is a complexion that appears more vibrant and rejuvenated, complementing the physical benefits of facial sculpting exercises.

To effectively strengthen the neck and complement facial sculpting, it is crucial to perform exercises that specifically target the neck muscles without straining them. Gentle stretches, isometric exercises, and movements that encourage the full range of motion of the neck are particularly beneficial. These exercises should be performed with careful attention to form and breathing, ensuring that each movement is deliberate and controlled. By doing so, individuals can maximize the benefits of neck exercises, improving both the appearance and function of the neck and facial muscles.

Incorporating neck exercises into a daily routine does not require a significant time commitment. Even a few minutes a day can lead to noticeable improvements over time. Consistency is key, as the cumulative effect of regular, targeted exercises can significantly enhance the results of facial sculpting efforts. As with any exercise routine, it is important to listen to the body and adjust the intensity and frequency of exercises to accommodate individual needs and goals.

Ultimately, the importance of strengthening the neck to complement facial sculpting cannot be overstated. By integrating neck exercises into a holistic approach to facial fitness, individuals can achieve a more balanced, youthful, and defined appearance. This comprehensive strategy not only enhances physical beauty but also promotes overall well-being, offering a natural and effective way to maintain a youthful look and boost confidence.

Neck Sagging and Facial Appearance

Sagging in the neck area, often perceived as a telltale sign of aging, can profoundly impact the overall facial appearance, subtly altering the perceived contours and symmetry of the face. This phenomenon, resulting from a combination of factors such as loss of skin elasticity, diminished muscle tone, and the gravitational pull over time, can lead to a less defined jawline, creating an impression of a double chin or a blurring of the neck and chin demarcation. The visual effect of neck sagging extends beyond the immediate area, influencing the harmony and youthful appearance of the entire face. As the skin and underlying muscles in the neck area begin to lose their firmness and resilience, the support they provide to facial structures diminishes, potentially leading to a downward shift in facial features and an overall drooping appearance. This can make the cheeks appear more prominent or saggy, and the lines around the mouth and nose more pronounced, contributing to a tired or aged look.

The psychological impact of these changes should not be underestimated. For many, the neck and jawline are symbols of vitality and youth, and changes in this area can affect self-perception and confidence. Recognizing the interconnectedness of facial and neck aesthetics is crucial in addressing these concerns. Strengthening and toning the muscles of the neck through targeted exercises can provide a natural lift to the area, subtly elevating the facial features and restoring a more youthful contour to the face. These exercises, by improving muscle tone and skin tightness, can counteract the effects of sagging and create a firmer, more defined neck and jawline, which in turn enhances the overall facial appearance.

Moreover, the skin's health plays a pivotal role in the appearance of the neck area. A regimen that includes hydration, proper nutrition, and skincare tailored to maintaining elasticity can complement physical exercises, creating a multifaceted approach to tackling neck sagging. This holistic strategy underscores the importance of a comprehensive approach to facial and neck aesthetics, emphasizing that improvements in the neck area can lead to significant enhancements in the overall facial appearance.

Incorporating these exercises and skincare practices into a daily routine requires minimal time investment yet yields substantial benefits. Regular engagement in a targeted neck and chin tightening regimen not only promises aesthetic improvements but also fosters a sense of agency over one's appearance and aging process. The act of dedicating time to self-care and physical maintenance can bolster self-esteem and contribute to a positive self-image, reinforcing the intrinsic link between physical appearance and psychological well-being.

The journey tc mitigating the effects of neck sagging and enhancing facial appearance is one of patience and consistency. It is a testament to the body's remarkable ability to respond to and benefit from focused care and exercise. By addressing neck sagging with the seriousness it deserves, individuals can achieve a harmonious, youthful appearance that reflects their inner vitality and confidence, proving that with the right approach, the challenges of aging can be met with grace and determination.

Improving Neck Flexibility and Tightness for Better Posture and Aesthetics

Improving neck flexibility and tightness is essential not only for enhancing your aesthetic appearance but also for promoting better posture and overall well-being. The neck plays a crucial role in supporting the head and maintaining alignment with the spine. When the neck is flexible and strong, it can help reduce tension and discomfort, leading to a more confident posture and a defined jawline.

Benefits of Neck Flexibility and Tightness

1. Enhanced Posture: A flexible neck allows for better alignment of the head over the spine, reducing the risk of slouching or hunching. This alignment is vital for maintaining a healthy posture, which can prevent long-term issues such as back pain and discomfort.

2. Reduced Neck Tension: Regularly engaging in neck flexibility exercises can alleviate tightness and tension that often accumulate due to stress, poor posture, or prolonged periods of sitting. This relief can lead to a more relaxed demeanor and improved overall comfort.

3. Aesthetic Improvements: A well-maintained neck contributes to a more youthful and defined facial appearance. By reducing excess tension and promoting flexibility, you can enhance the contours of your jawline and neck, creating a more sculpted look.

4. Increased Range of Motion: Improved flexibility in the neck allows for a greater range of motion, making everyday activities more comfortable and reducing the risk of injury during physical activities.

5. Boosted Confidence: With better posture and a more defined appearance, you may find yourself feeling more confident in social situations and daily interactions. This boost in self-esteem can have a positive impact on various aspects of your life.

Incorporating neck flexibility and tightness exercises into your daily routine can yield significant benefits for both your posture and aesthetic appearance. By dedicating just a few minutes each day to these exercises, you can work towards a healthier, more confident you.

Exercises: Explanations and Benefits

Neck Stretch

Purpose: To improve neck flexibility and posture while reducing tension in the neck and shoulders, contributing to a more defined jawline and overall facial aesthetics.

Target Area: Cervical spine muscles, focusing on enhancing flexibility and strength for better posture and facial structure support.

Step-by-Step Instructions

Starting Position: Sit in a comfortable chair with your feet flat on the ground, back straight, and shoulders relaxed. Keep your head in a neutral position, eyes looking forward.

Movement:

1. Forward Neck Stretch:

- Gently lower your chin towards your chest, aiming to stretch the back of your neck
- Hold this position for 5-10 seconds, feeling a gentle stretch along the back of your neck
- Slowly lift your head back to the neutral starting position

2. Lateral Neck Stretch:

- Tilt your head to the right, bringing your ear towards your shoulder without lifting the shoulder

- Extend your right arm and place your hand over the left side of your head, applying gentle pressure to deepen the stretch
- Hold for 5-10 seconds, then gently release and return to the starting position
- Repeat on the left side, tilting your head to the left and using your left hand

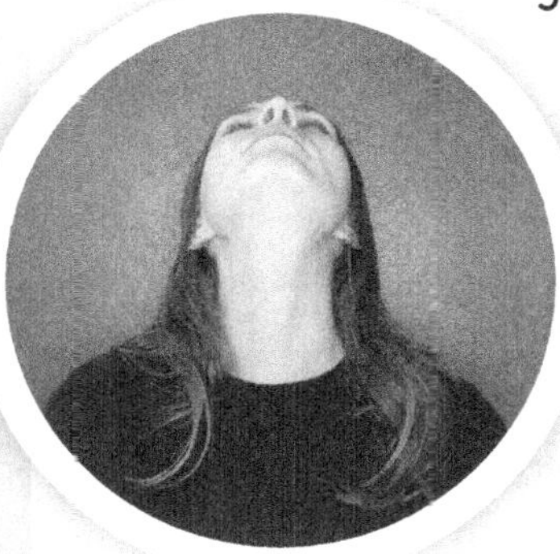

3. Neck Extension:

- Gently tilt your head backward, looking up at the ceiling. This stretches the front of your neck
- Hold for 5-10 seconds, then carefully return to the neutral starting position

Duration/ Repetitions: Perform each stretch 10 times, holding each for 5-10 seconds. Aim for 2-3 sets throughout the day for optimal results

Pro Tips

- Ensure movements are slow and controlled to prevent any strain or injury
- Focus on maintaining a relaxed breathing pattern throughout the exercises to enhance the stretching effect
- Adjust the pressure and range of motion according to your comfort level; the stretches should feel good and not cause pain

Common Mistakes to Avoid

- Avoid shrugging your shoulders up towards your ears during the stretches; keep your shoulders relaxed and down
- Do not apply excessive pressure with your hand during lateral stretches; the goal is gentle tension, not force
- Ensure you do not hold your breath; maintaining a steady, relaxed breathing pattern is crucial for relaxation and effectiveness.

Neck Rotations

Purpose: To improve neck flexibility, relieve tension, and enhance overall facial appearance by promoting better posture.

Target Area: Neck and upper back.

Step-by-Step Instructions

Starting Position: Begin in a comfortable seated position with your back straight and shoulders relaxed.

Movement:

1. Slowly turn your head to the right, aiming to look over your right shoulder as far as feels comfortable
2. Hold this position for 5-10 seconds, allowing the muscles in your neck to stretch and relax
3. Gradually return your head to the center, taking a moment to reset your posture

4. Now, repeat the rotation to the left side, turning your head to look over your left shoulder
5. Hold for 5-10 seconds, feeling the stretch along the side of your neck
6. Return to the center once more, ensuring your movements remain slow and controlled throughout the exercise

Duration/ Repetitions: Perform the neck rotation 10 times on each side, holding each position for 5-10 seconds. Aim for 2-3 sets throughout the day to maximize benefits.

Pro Tips

- Keep your shoulders relaxed and down during the rotation to avoid tension.
- Focus on your breathing, inhaling deeply and exhaling slowly to enhance relaxation.
- Adjust the range of motion according to your comfort level, ensuring the movement feels good.

Common Mistakes to Avoid

- Do not rush through the rotations; maintain a steady pace to prevent strain.
- Avoid holding your breath; a relaxed breathing pattern is essential for effectiveness.
- Ensure you do not lean forward or backward while rotating; keep your head aligned with your spine.

Collarbone Sculptor

Purpose: To sculpt and define the collarbone area while enhancing neck muscle tone, contributing to a more elegant neck and shoulder line.

Target Area: Sternocleidomastoid and platysma muscles, focusing on the area around the collarbones and the front of the neck.

Step-by-Step Instructions

Starting Position: Sit or stand with your back straight and shoulders pulled back slightly to open up the chest. Keep your head level and your gaze forward.

Movement:

1. Extend your neck slightly by tilting your head back, aiming to create a gentle stretch in the front of your neck.
2. With your lips closed and teeth slightly apart, smile as wide as you can to engage the muscles around your collarbone and neck.
3. Place your fingertips gently on the collarbones to feel the muscle engagement and ensure the focus remains on this area.
4. Hold the smile and the neck extension for 5-10 seconds, keeping the rest of your body relaxed.
5. Slowly return to the starting position, relaxing the smile and bringing your head back to a neutral position.
6. Repeat this movement 10 times for one set.

Duration/ Repetitions: Hold each position for 5-10 seconds. Perform 10 repetitions per set, aiming for 2-3 sets.

Pro Tips

- Ensure that your shoulders remain pulled back and down throughout the exercise to maximize engagement around the collarbones.
- Focus on creating a wide, genuine smile to effectively engage the muscles without straining the neck.
- Breathe normally throughout the exercise to maintain relaxation and proper muscle function.

Common Mistakes to Avoid

- Avoid lifting your shoulders towards your ears, as this can create tension in the neck and shoulders, reducing the effectiveness of the exercise.
- Do not overextend your neck or force the smile, as this can lead to strain. The movement should be comfortable and controlled.
- Ensure not to hold your breath; maintaining a steady breathing pattern is crucial for relaxation and effectiveness.

Chapter 7

Wrinkle Prevention Techniques

Facial Exercises and Wrinkle Prevention

Facial exercises, when performed correctly, can be a powerful tool in maintaining a youthful appearance, enhancing facial contours, and promoting skin elasticity. However, it's crucial to acknowledge that improper technique can inadvertently lead to wrinkle formation. This paradox arises because the skin on our face is delicate and susceptible to stretching and creasing, especially when subjected to repeated movements in an incorrect manner. To navigate this, understanding the mechanics of facial movements and adopting precise techniques is essential.

Firstly, it's important to differentiate between muscle strengthening and skin stretching. Effective facial exercises target the muscles beneath the skin, aiming to tone and lift without excessively pulling or stretching the skin's surface. This distinction is vital because while we want to engage and strengthen facial muscles, we must ensure that the skin itself is not being overworked or strained. To achieve this, exercises should be performed with a focus on gentle muscle engagement, avoiding any movements that pull or distort the skin excessively.

One common mistake leading to wrinkle formation is applying too much force or using incorrect facial expressions during exercises. For instance, overly exaggerated movements can stretch the skin too much, creating fine lines over time. To prevent this, exercises should be done in front of a mirror initially to monitor and correct any excessive skin movement. This practice helps in maintaining a soft and relaxed facial expression, ensuring that the skin is not being unduly stretched.

Another key aspect is the integration of relaxation techniques into your facial exercise routine. Just as with any other form of exercise, allowing the muscles to relax and recover is crucial. Incorporating moments of relaxation helps in releasing any built-up tension, which, if left unchecked, can contribute to the formation of expression lines and wrinkles. Techniques such as deep breathing, gentle facial massage, or applying a warm cloth to the face can aid in muscle relaxation, enhancing the overall effectiveness of your routine while safeguarding against wrinkle formation.

Hydration, both internal and external, plays a supportive role in wrinkle prevention. Well-hydrated skin maintains its elasticity more effectively, reducing the likelihood of creasing during exercises. Therefore, complementing your facial workout with a consistent hydration routine—drinking ample water and using hydrating skincare products—can provide a protective barrier against potential skin damage.

Lastly, the gradual progression of exercises is fundamental. Just as you would not start with heavy weights in a traditional workout, similarly, facial exercises should begin gently, gradually increasing in intensity as your muscles adapt. This approach not only prevents muscle strain but also minimizes the risk of inadvertently stretching the skin.

By adhering to these guidelines—focusing on gentle, precise movements, incorporating relaxation and hydration, and gradually progressing in intensity—facial exercises can indeed be a safe and effective method to enhance facial aesthetics without the unintended consequence of wrinkle formation. This careful balance ensures that the pursuit of a toned, youthful appearance remains both a healthy and attainable goal.

How to Strengthen Muscles Without Creating Creases or Wrinkles

Strengthening facial muscles is essential for maintaining a youthful appearance, but it is equally important to do so in a way that minimizes the risk of developing creases or wrinkles. The key lies in understanding the anatomy of the face and employing techniques that focus on muscle engagement without overstretching the skin.

Understanding Facial Muscles

The face is composed of various muscles that work together to create expressions. Key muscle groups include the orbicularis oris around the mouth, the zygomaticus major and minor in the cheeks, and the orbicularis oculi around the eyes. By targeting these muscles specifically, you can enhance their strength and tone while avoiding unnecessary strain on the skin.

Effective Techniques for Muscle Strengthening

1. Isolated Movements: Focus on exercises that isolate specific muscle groups. This prevents the engagement of surrounding muscles that could lead to unwanted tension and skin creasing. For example, when working on cheek muscles, ensure that the lower part of your face remains relaxed.

2. Gentle Touch: When using your fingers to guide muscle engagement, apply a gentle touch. Pressing too hard can create pressure lines and contribute to skin sagging over time. A light touch allows you to feel the muscles working without adding stress to the skin.

3. Mindful Expression: Maintain a neutral expression when transitioning between exercises. This helps to avoid unnecessary movement in areas that are not being targeted, reducing the risk of developing fine lines.

4. Breathing Techniques: Incorporate deep, even breathing throughout your routine. This not only enhances relaxation but also helps to keep your facial muscles loose and free from tension, which is crucial for preventing wrinkles.

5. Mirror Practice: Utilize a mirror to observe your facial movements. This allows you to ensure that you are not inadvertently creating tension in other areas of your face while focusing on the targeted muscles.

Common Pitfalls to Avoid

- Overstretching the skin during exercises can lead to permanent creases, so always be mindful of your movements
- Holding your breath can create tension, so focus on maintaining a steady breathing pattern
- Pressing too firmly with your fingers can create pressure lines, so keep your touch light and gentle

By following these guidelines, you can effectively strengthen your facial muscles while minimizing the risk of creating creases or wrinkles, ensuring a smoother and more youthful appearance as you progress in your facial shaping journey.

Muscle Relaxation and Stretching Post-Exercise

Muscle relaxation and stretching post-exercise play a pivotal role in the overall effectiveness and safety of your facial workout regimen. Just as cooling down is a non-negotiable part of a traditional physical workout, similarly, allowing your facial muscles to relax after a series of exercises is crucial for preventing muscle tension, which can lead to unnecessary stress on your skin and the formation of fine lines. This section delves into practical strategies to ensure that your facial muscles are adequately relaxed and stretched, paving the way for a more toned and youthful appearance without the adverse effects of muscle strain or skin creasing.

Firstly, incorporating gentle facial massages into your post-exercise routine can significantly enhance muscle relaxation. Using the tips of your fingers, apply light pressure in circular motions across different areas of your face. This not only helps in relieving any built-up tension in the muscles but also promotes blood circulation, contributing to skin health and elasticity. Focus on areas that are particularly prone to tension, such as the jawline, forehead, and around the eyes, ensuring a thorough and relaxing massage that leaves your facial muscles feeling eased and rejuvenated.

Another effective technique for post-exercise muscle relaxation is the application of a warm compress. The warmth helps in relaxing the muscles further and can be particularly soothing if you've engaged in intensive exercises. Simply soak a clean cloth in warm water, wring out the excess, and gently place it over your face for a few minutes. This not only aids in muscle relaxation but also opens up the pores, making it a perfect precursor to applying moisturizer or serum, thereby enhancing the absorption of skincare products.

Stretching is equally important and can be done through simple exercises that target the relaxation of facial muscles. For instance, yawning exercises are excellent for releasing tension in the jaw and neck. Open your mouth wide, as if yawning, and hold the position for a few seconds before releasing. Repeat several times to ensure the muscles around your jaw and neck are adequately stretched and relaxed. Similarly, gentle eye exercises, like closing your eyes tightly and then opening them wide, can help in relaxing the muscles around your eyes, reducing the risk of crow's feet and under-eye wrinkles.

Breathing exercises also complement the muscle relaxation process effectively. Deep, slow breathing not only aids in relaxing the mind and body but also ensures that oxygen is efficiently circulated to your facial muscles, aiding in their recovery and relaxation. Incorporate deep breathing exercises at the end of your facial workout, focusing on inhaling deeply through the nose and exhaling slowly through the mouth. This not only helps in muscle relaxation but also instills a sense of calm and readiness to proceed with your day or night skincare routine.

Lastly, hydration plays a crucial role in muscle relaxation. Drinking plenty of water throughout the day and especially after your facial exercises helps in maintaining muscle flexibility and skin elasticity. Well-hydrated muscles are more resilient and recover more efficiently, reducing the likelihood of tension buildup. Additionally, applying a hydrating moisturizer or serum post-exercise can lock in moisture, further supporting the skin's recovery process and ensuring that your facial muscles remain relaxed and well-nourished.

By integrating these muscle relaxation and stretching techniques into your post-exercise routine, you not only enhance the effectiveness of your facial workouts but also contribute significantly to the longevity of your skin's health and appearance. These practices ensure that your pursuit of a toned and youthful facial contour is achieved in the most gentle and nurturing way possible, aligning with your overall wellness and skincare goals.

Skincare and Hydration for Facial Fitness

To complement the benefits of facial exercises and further enhance the results, incorporating a dedicated skincare and hydration routine is essential. Skincare routines tailored to your skin type and concerns can significantly amplify the effects of your facial workouts, leading to more pronounced and lasting results. This section will guide you through establishing a skincare regimen that not only supports but also maximizes the benefits of your facial fitness journey.

Firstly, cleansing is the cornerstone of any effective skincare routine. Starting and ending your day with a gentle cleanser removes impurities and prepares your skin for the subsequent steps in your regimen. Opt for a cleanser that matches your skin type—whether it be oily, dry, combination, or sensitive—to ensure that your skin is thoroughly cleansed without stripping it of its natural oils.

Following cleansing, toning helps to balance the skin's pH levels, refine pores, and better prepare the skin for the absorption of moisturizers and serums. A hydrating toner, particularly those containing ingredients like hyaluronic acid or glycerin, can provide an additional layer of moisture, crucial for maintaining skin elasticity and plumpness.

Serums are potent formulations designed to target specific skin concerns, such as fine lines, uneven skin tone, or dehydration. Incorporating a serum into your routine can significantly enhance your skin's health and appearance. For those focusing on facial exercises, serums with collagen-boosting, firming, or hydrating properties can be particularly beneficial. These concentrated products support the skin's structure, aiding in the firming and toning process initiated by your exercises.

Moisturizing is a step that cannot be overlooked. A good moisturizer not only locks in the benefits of the previous steps but also ensures that your skin remains hydrated and nourished. For daytime, opt for a lighter formula that includes SPF to protect against sun damage, a critical factor in maintaining skin health and preventing premature aging. In the evening, a more nourishing cream can be used to support the skin's natural repair processes overnight.

Sun protection is vital in preventing skin damage and aging. Daily use of a broad-spectrum sunscreen protects against the harmful effects of UV radiation, preserving your skin's elasticity and firmness. This step is crucial, as sun damage can counteract the benefits of facial exercises by breaking down collagen and causing skin laxity.

Hydration plays a dual role in supporting facial fitness. Internally, drinking adequate amounts of water is essential for maintaining overall health and ensuring that your skin is well-hydrated from the inside out. Aim for at least 8 glasses of water a day, or more if you're active or live in a hot climate. Externally, using hydrating skincare products helps to maintain the skin's moisture barrier, improving elasticity and smoothness. Look for products containing ingredients known for their hydrating properties, such as hyaluronic acid, aloe vera, or squalane.

Finally, incorporating a weekly exfoliation into your routine can help to remove dead skin cells, promoting cell turnover and revealing a brighter, more even complexion. However, it's important to choose a gentle exfoliant and not over-exfoliate, as this can lead to irritation and compromise the skin's barrier function.

By integrating these skincare and hydration practices into your daily routine, you create a supportive environment for your facial exercises to thrive. This holistic approach not only enhances the visible results of your workouts but also contributes to the overall health and vitality of your skin, ensuring that your efforts lead to a more youthful, radiant complexion.

Chapter 8

Goal-Based Facial Routines

Customizing Routines for Facial Goals

Creating a facial exercise routine that aligns with your specific goals requires a strategic approach, one that considers the unique contours, strengths, and areas of concern within your facial structure. Whether your aim is to diminish the appearance of a double chin, sculpt a more defined jawline, or enhance the overall tone and firmness of your face, the key lies in selecting exercises that target these objectives effectively. This process begins with a clear assessment of your facial features and identifying the areas you wish to improve. From there, you can construct a personalized routine that not only addresses your concerns but also complements the natural shape and symmetry of your face.

For those looking to reduce a double chin, exercises that focus on the lower face and neck, such as the Chin Lift and Neck Resistance Push, can be particularly beneficial. These exercises are designed to engage and strengthen the muscles beneath the chin and along the neck, promoting a more contoured and lifted appearance over time. Incorporating these exercises into your daily routine, with careful attention to technique and form, can help in gradually reducing the appearance of submental fat and enhancing the definition of your jawline.

If sculpting a more defined jawline is your primary goal, prioritizing exercises like the Jawline Sculptor and Jaw Clenches can yield significant results. These movements target the muscles around the jaw and cheeks, building strength and definition in these areas. By focusing on exercises that enhance the contour and definition of the jawline, you can work towards achieving a more sculpted and youthful facial profile. It's important to perform these exercises with precision, ensuring that each movement is executed with control to maximize engagement and effectiveness.

For individuals aiming to improve the overall tone and firmness of their face, incorporating a variety of exercises that target different facial muscles is essential. A balanced routine that includes the Cheek Lift, Forehead Smoother, and Eye Area Lift can help in evenly toning the face, promoting a more lifted and youthful appearance. These exercises work together to strengthen and tighten the facial muscles, supporting skin elasticity and reducing the appearance of sagging or drooping. By engaging in a comprehensive facial workout that addresses multiple areas, you can enhance facial symmetry and achieve a more balanced and harmonious look.

In addition to selecting the right exercises, consistency is paramount in achieving and maintaining results. Committing to a daily routine, even on busy days, ensures that your facial muscles are regularly engaged and strengthened. This consistent effort is crucial in gradually sculpting and toning the face, leading to visible improvements over time. Furthermore, integrating these exercises into your daily activities, such as while watching TV or during your skincare routine, can make it easier to maintain consistency without disrupting your schedule.

Finally, listening to your body and adjusting your routine as needed is essential for safe and effective facial toning. If you experience discomfort or strain in certain areas, it may be necessary to modify the intensity or frequency of specific exercises. Paying attention to how your face responds to the exercises allows you to tailor your routine more effectively, ensuring that you achieve your desired outcomes without compromising your skin's health or comfort.

By thoughtfully customizing your facial exercise routine based on your specific goals, and approaching your practice with consistency, precision, and mindfulness, you can effectively enhance your facial contours, improve muscle tone, and achieve a more youthful and radiant appearance. This personalized approach not only addresses your unique concerns but also empowers you to take control of your facial fitness journey, leading to lasting results and boosted confidence.

Identify Target Areas & Set Realistic Goals

Identifying your target areas and setting realistic goals is a pivotal step in customizing a facial exercise routine that aligns with your aspirations for a more defined and youthful appearance. This process begins with a thorough assessment of your facial structure to pinpoint specific areas that you feel could benefit from toning and sculpting. Perhaps you've noticed a slight sagging along the jawline, or maybe the area under your chin doesn't feel as firm as you'd like it to be. It could also be that you're looking to enhance the overall firmness of your face to achieve a more radiant and lifted look. Whatever your areas of concern may be, recognizing them is the first step towards making targeted improvements.

Once you've identified these areas, the next step is to set achievable goals. It's important to approach this with a sense of realism, understanding that while facial exercises can produce noticeable changes, these changes will not appear overnight. Setting goals such as "I want to reduce the appearance of my double chin within the next three months" or "I aim to enhance the definition of my jawline over the next six weeks" provides you with a clear target to work towards. These goals should be specific, measurable, achievable, relevant, and time-bound (SMART), ensuring that you have a clear path forward and can track your progress effectively.

Achieving these goals requires consistency and dedication to your facial exercise routine. Incorporating exercises that specifically target your areas of concern is crucial. For instance, if your goal is to reduce a double chin, focusing on exercises like the Chin Lift and Neck Resistance Push will be key. Similarly, if you're aiming to sculpt a more defined jawline, incorporating the Jawline Sculptor and Jaw Clenches into your daily routine will help you work towards this goal. It's also beneficial to include a variety of exercises that target different facial muscles to ensure a balanced and holistic approach to facial toning. This not only helps in achieving your specific goals but also contributes to the overall vitality and youthfulness of your face.

In addition to the exercises themselves, paying attention to technique is paramount. Proper execution ensures that you're engaging the right muscles and maximizing the effectiveness of each movement without risking injury or discomfort. It's also worth noting that while dedication to your routine is important, listening to your body is equally crucial. If you experience any pain or discomfort, adjusting the intensity or frequency of your exercises may be necessary. This mindful approach ensures that you're not only working towards your aesthetic goals but also prioritizing your health and well-being in the process.

Furthermore, integrating these exercises into your daily routine in a way that feels seamless and manageable is essential for long-term success. Whether it's performing a few exercises in the morning as part of your skincare routine or taking a few minutes to engage in facial toning before bed, finding moments throughout your day to dedicate to your facial fitness can make a significant difference in your progress. This consistent effort, combined with a positive and patient mindset, will pave the way for noticeable improvements in your facial tone and contour.

By identifying your target areas, setting realistic goals, and approaching your facial exercise routine with consistency, precision, and care, you're not just working towards enhancing your appearance. You're also embracing a practice that promotes self-care and well-being, leading to not only a more sculpted and youthful face but also a deeper sense of confidence and satisfaction with your self-image. This journey, while focused on achieving specific aesthetic goals, is ultimately a celebration of your commitment to self-improvement and the remarkable capabilities of your body to transform and rejuvenate itself through dedicated effort and care.

Efficient Exercise Routine Creation

Crafting an efficient routine that synergizes different facial exercises requires a strategic approach, ensuring that each session maximizes the potential for toning and sculpting the face while being mindful of the time constraints and lifestyle of a busy, health-conscious woman. The key to success lies in the thoughtful combination of exercises that target various facial areas, allowing for a comprehensive workout that addresses all your facial fitness goals without overburdening your schedule. This method not only promotes a harmonious facial symmetry but also ensures that you're engaging in a sustainable practice, fitting seamlessly into your daily life.

To begin, select a core set of exercises from the chapters dedicated to double chin reduction, jawline sculpting, and full-face toning. This selection should reflect your primary goals, whether they're focused on diminishing the appearance of a double chin, defining your jawline, or enhancing the overall firmness of your face. For instance, if your aim is to sculpt a more defined jawline while also targeting a double chin, incorporating exercises like the Chin Lift, Jawline Sculptor, and Neck Resistance Push into your routine provides a targeted approach to these areas.

Once you've identified these core exercises, the next step is to integrate additional movements that complement your main goals and contribute to full-face toning. This might include exercises like the Cheek Lift and Eye Area Lift, which support skin elasticity and add to the sculpting effect by targeting the upper and mid-face areas. The inclusion of these exercises ensures a balanced workout that prevents the overdevelopment of certain muscles and promotes a more youthful, lifted appearance across the entire face.

The art of combining these exercises into a cohesive routine involves alternating between different muscle groups to allow for adequate rest and recovery. For example, after performing an exercise that intensely targets the jawline, follow it with a gentler exercise focused on the eye area or cheeks. This strategy not only prevents muscle fatigue but also keeps the workout engaging and dynamic, reducing the risk of boredom and ensuring that you remain committed to your facial fitness journey.

Timing and sequence play a crucial role in the effectiveness of your routine. Begin with a warm-up using gentle facial movements to increase circulation and prepare the muscles for more intensive exercises. Following the warm-up, move on to the more demanding exercises that require higher muscle engagement, ensuring that these are performed when your muscles are most receptive. Conclude with cooling down exercises that promote relaxation and muscle recovery, such as gentle facial massages or stretches. This structured approach maximizes the benefits of each session, enhancing muscle tone and skin elasticity while minimizing the risk of strain or injury.

Incorporating these exercises into your daily routine can be made more manageable by identifying moments throughout your day that lend themselves to brief workout sessions. Morning routines, while applying skincare products, or evening rituals before bed, offer perfect opportunities to engage in facial exercises. Even short sessions, when performed consistently, can lead to significant improvements over time.

Adjusting the intensity and duration of your exercises based on your progress and any feedback from your body is essential. If you notice discomfort or fatigue, it may be necessary to scale back and focus on fewer exercises, gradually increasing the intensity as your strength and endurance improve. This adaptive approach ensures that your routine remains effective and enjoyable, aligning with your evolving facial fitness goals and personal lifestyle.

By meticulously selecting and combining facial exercises into an efficient routine, you're not just working towards enhancing your physical appearance; you're also embracing a practice that nurtures your well-being and self-confidence. This personalized, goal-oriented approach to facial fitness empowers you to achieve a toned, youthful complexion, reflecting your dedication to self-care and your commitment to a healthier, more vibrant you.

Adjusting Your Routine as You See Results

As you embark on this transformative journey with facial exercises, observing and responding to the changes in your facial structure is paramount. The beauty of a personalized facial fitness routine lies in its flexibility to evolve as you progress, ensuring that the exercises remain effective and aligned with your evolving goals. Recognizing the signs of improvement requires a keen eye for detail and an understanding of the nuances of your facial anatomy. As muscles become more toned and the skin appears firmer, it may be time to adjust the intensity, frequency, or specific exercises within your routine to continue challenging your facial muscles and prevent plateauing.

Initially, the focus might have been on reducing a double chin or sculpting the jawline, with exercises selected specifically for these purposes. However, as these areas begin to show signs of improvement, it becomes essential to reassess your goals and consider incorporating exercises that target other areas of the face or increase the complexity of your current routine. For instance, if the jawline becomes more defined, adding exercises that enhance cheekbones or tighten the forehead might be the next step in achieving a balanced and harmonious facial appearance.

Adjusting your routine is not solely about adding new exercises; it also involves modifying the intensity and duration of your current exercises. As your facial muscles grow stronger, they require more resistance or longer durations to continue developing. This might mean increasing the number of repetitions, extending the duration of each exercise, or incorporating resistance tools, such as facial exercise bands, to provide additional challenge.

Moreover, the frequency of your routine may need modification. In the early stages, daily exercises might have been necessary to kickstart muscle toning and fat reduction. However, as you progress, your muscles will need more time to recover and rebuild, potentially leading to a routine that alternates between intensive exercise days and rest or maintenance days. This balance ensures that you continue to see results without overworking the muscles or causing strain.

Listening to your body remains a critical aspect of adjusting your routine. Pay attention to signs of fatigue or strain, which may indicate the need for a rest day or a reduction in exercise intensity. Conversely, if exercises become too comfortable or no longer provide a challenge, it's a clear signal to increase the difficulty level. Keeping a detailed exercise journal can be incredibly helpful in this process, allowing you to track your progress, note any changes in how the exercises feel, and adjust your routine based on empirical evidence of what works best for you.

Finally, integrating advanced techniques or focusing on precision and mindfulness during each exercise can further enhance your results. As you become more experienced, paying close attention to the execution of each movement, ensuring proper form, and fully engaging the targeted muscles can make even familiar exercises more effective. This advanced approach maximizes the benefits of each session, encouraging continued improvement and helping you achieve and maintain the youthful, radiant complexion that reflects your dedication to facial fitness.

In essence, the journey of facial toning is ongoing, with each phase offering new opportunities for growth and refinement. By staying attuned to the changes in your facial structure, being willing to adapt your routine, and embracing the challenges of more advanced exercises, you ensure that your facial fitness journey is not only successful but also rewarding and sustainable over the long term.

Routines

Routine 1: Double Chin Reduction Routine (< 5 minutes)

Purpose: To target and reduce the appearance of a double chin by strengthening and toning the muscles around the jawline and under the chin.

Target Area: Platysma muscle, jawline, and under-chin area.

Step-by-Step Instructions:

Starting Position: Sit or stand with your back straight, shoulders relaxed, and head in a neutral position, looking forward.

Movement:

1. **Warm-Up Neck Rotations:**
    - Gently turn your head to the right, aiming to align your chin with your shoulder.
    - Hold for a moment, then slowly rotate to the left side.
    - Perform this rotation 5 times on each side to loosen the neck muscles.
2. **Chin Lift:**
    - Tilt your head back to look at the ceiling.
    - Pucker your lips as if you are trying to kiss the ceiling, creating a stretch in the area under your chin.
    - Hold this position for 5 seconds.
    - Repeat 5 times.
3. **Tongue Stretch:**
    - Keep your head in a neutral position, looking forward.
    - Stick your tongue out as far as possible, trying to reach your chin with the tip of your tongue.
    - Hold this stretch for 5 seconds.
    - Repeat 5 times.
4. **Jaw Jut:**
    - Tilt your head back, looking at the ceiling.
    - Slide your lower jaw forward until you feel a stretch under your chin.

- Hold this position for 5 seconds.
- Return to the starting position and repeat 5 times.

5. **Neck Resistance Push:**
    - Place one hand on your forehead.
    - Push your head against your hand without allowing your head to move forward.
    - Hold this resistance for 5-10 seconds.
    - Repeat 5 times, then switch to placing your hand on the back of your head and pushing backward, repeating the resistance push 5 times.

Duration/ Repetitions: Complete each exercise with the recommended repetitions and hold times, aiming for a total routine duration of about 5 minutes.

Pro Tips

- Focus on maintaining a relaxed breathing pattern throughout the exercises to enhance muscle relaxation and effectiveness.
- Ensure smooth, controlled movements to avoid strain, particularly during the neck rotations and jaw jut exercises.
- For the neck resistance push, apply steady pressure without causing discomfort or pain.

Common Mistakes to Avoid

- Avoid straining your neck by overextending during the chin lift and jaw jut exercises.
- Do not hold your breath while performing these exercises; proper breathing is crucial for relaxation and effectiveness.
- Ensure not to use too much force during the neck resistance push to prevent neck strain.

Estimated Time: Approximately 5 minutes for the complete routine.

Routine 2: Jawline Sculpting Routine (< 5 minutes)

Purpose: To sculpt and define the jawline by targeting the muscles around the jaw and neck for a more toned and youthful appearance.

Target Area: Masseter muscle, mandible contour, and platysma muscle.

Step-by-Step Instructions:

Starting Position: Sit in an upright position with your back straight and shoulders relaxed. Keep your head level and your gaze forward to ensure proper alignment of the neck and spine.

Movement:

1. **Jaw Clenches:**
    - With your mouth closed, clench your teeth gently and feel the tension build in your jaw muscles.
    - Hold this clench for 3-5 seconds, then release gently.
    - Repeat 10 times.
2. **Jaw Push-Ups:**
    - Place your palms gently on the sides of your jaw, applying light resistance.
    - Open your mouth slowly against the resistance of your hands, then close it.
    - Perform 10 repetitions.
3. **Cheek Lift:**
    - Smile as wide as you can, trying to lift the corners of your mouth towards your ears.
    - Place your fingertips on your cheeks to feel the muscles engage.
    - Hold the smile for 5 seconds, then relax.
    - Repeat 5 times.
4. **Fish Face:**
    - Suck in your cheeks and lips to make a fish face, creating tension in the cheeks and jaw.
    - Hold this position for 5 seconds before releasing.
    - Repeat 5 times.

5. **The V Shape:**
    - With your mouth closed, try to smile while keeping your teeth hidden. You should feel a slight pull at the corners of your mouth.
    - Using your index fingers, lightly push up the corners of your lips to deepen the V shape.
    - Hold for 5 seconds, then release.
    - Repeat 5 times.

Duration/ Repetitions: The entire routine should take approximately 5 minutes to complete, with each exercise performed in sets of 10 repetitions.

Pro Tips

- Focus on engaging the muscles with precision rather than using force, especially when applying resistance with your hands.
- Maintain a relaxed breathing pattern throughout the exercises to enhance muscle engagement and relaxation.
- Use a mirror to monitor your technique and ensure that you are isolating the correct muscles without straining other areas of your face.

Common Mistakes to Avoid

- Avoid over-clenching your teeth during jaw clenches to prevent jaw pain or discomfort.
- Do not apply too much pressure with your hands during jaw push-ups the goal is gentle resistance.
- Ensure not to hold your breath while performing the exercises; proper oxygenation is crucial for muscle function and recovery.

Estimated Time: 5 minutes for the complete routine, making it ideal for daily practice to achieve a sculpted and defined jawline.

Routine 3: Anti-Wrinkle and Skin Tightening Routine (< 5 minutes)

Purpose: To minimize the appearance of wrinkles and tighten the skin through targeted facial muscle exercises, promoting a smoother and more youthful complexion.

Target Area: This routine focuses on the orbicularis oris (around the mouth), zygomaticus major and minor (cheek muscles), orbicularis oculi (around the eyes), and the forehead muscles.

Step-by-Step Instructions

Starting Position: Begin seated or standing with a straight spine, shoulders down and relaxed. Ensure your face is in a neutral position, with no pre-existing tension in the muscles.

Movement:

1. **Forehead Smoother:**
    - Place your fingertips lightly across your forehead.
    - Gently sweep your fingers outward towards your temples, applying light pressure to smooth the skin.
    - Repeat 10 times.
2. **Eye Area Lift:**
    - Place your index fingers under each eye, pointing towards your nose.
    - Perform a gentle upward flick motion, lifting the skin slightly and then releasing.
    - Repeat 10 times.
3. **Cheek Puff:**
    - Take a deep breath through your mouth, filling your cheeks with air to puff them out.
    - Hold the air in your right cheek for 5 seconds, then switch to your left cheek for 5 seconds.
    - Release the air and relax.
    - Repeat 5 times.
4. **Smile Line Reducer:**
    - Smile as wide as you can while keeping your mouth closed.

- Place your fingertips on the smile lines (nasolabial folds) and gently glide them up towards your nose to smooth out the lines.
- Repeat 10 times.

5. **Crow's Feet Smoother:**
    - Gently place your fingertips at the outer corners of your eyes.
    - With a light touch, sweep your fingers up and out towards your temples, aiming to smooth out the crow's feet.
    - Repeat for 1 minute

Duration/ Repetitions: The entire routine should take approximately 5 minutes, with each exercise performed in the recommended repetitions.

Pro Tips

- Ensure your hands are clean and your skin is moisturized before starting the routine to prevent irritation and enhance the smooth gliding of your fingers on your skin.
- Focus on gentle movements to avoid pulling or dragging the skin, which could potentially contribute to more wrinkles.
- Incorporate deep, relaxed breathing throughout the routine to enhance muscle relaxation and overall effectiveness.

Common Mistakes to Avoid

- Applying too much pressure with your fingers, which can stretch the skin and counteract the benefits of the exercises.
- Rushing through the exercises without giving each muscle group the attention it needs.
- Holding your breath or tensing other parts of your face while performing the exercises, which can create unwanted tension and wrinkles.

Estimated Time: 5 minutes for the complete routine.

Routine 4: Full-Face Toning Routine for Busy Days (< 5 minutes)

Purpose: To offer a quick, comprehensive facial toning routine that can be easily integrated into a busy schedule, focusing on enhancing overall facial muscle tone for a more youthful appearance

Target Area: This routine targets multiple facial areas including the forehead, eyes, cheeks, jawline, and neck to provide balanced, full-face toning

Step-by-Step Instructions

Starting Position: Begin in a seated or standing position with your back straight, shoulders relaxed, and face in a neutral expression. Take a few deep breaths to center yourself before starting

Movement:

1. **Mid-Face Smoother:**
    - Open your mouth slightly and pull your lips inward to cover your teeth, creating an 'O' shape with your mouth.
    - Attempt to smile widely while keeping your lips over your teeth, feeling a stretch in your cheeks and around your mouth.
    - Place your fingers lightly on your cheeks, applying gentle pressure to create resistance against the smiling motion.
    - Hold this position for 5 seconds, focusing on the tension in your mid-face muscles.
    - Relax your smile and remove your fingers, returning to the starting position.
    - Repeat the movement 5 times.
2. **Under-Eye Smoother:**
    - Use your ring fingers (they apply the least pressure) to gently tap along the natural curve under your lower eyelids.
    - Start from the inner corners of your eyes and move outward toward your temples.
    - Repeat the tapping motion in a steady, rhythmic pattern for about 15 seconds.

   - After tapping, lightly sweep your fingers outward along the same path to promote lymphatic drainage.
   - Repeat this sequence 3 times.

3. **Ceiling Pout:**
   - Tilt your head back gently until you are comfortably looking at the ceiling
   - Push your lower jaw forward to feel a stretch under your chin and along your jawline
   - Hold this position and form an exaggerated pout with your lips
   - Maintain the pouted position while breathing comfortably
   - Keep the position for 20-30 seconds
4. **Jaw Release:**
   - Open your mouth wide as if yawning, feeling the stretch in your jaw
   - Hold this position for 5 seconds, then relax
   - Repeat this exercise 5 times
5. **Neck Stretch:**
   - Gently tilt your head to the right, bringing your ear towards your shoulder
   - Hold for 5 seconds, then return to center and repeat on the left side
   - Perform this stretch 5 times on each side

Duration/ Repetitions: The entire routine should take approximately 5 minutes, with each exercise performed for the recommended number of repetitions.

Pro Tips

- Ensure your movements are gentle to avoid pulling the skin, which can contribute to wrinkles.
- Focus on breathing deeply and evenly throughout the routine to enhance relaxation and muscle engagement.
- Use a mirror to monitor your technique, ensuring you are engaging the correct muscles without creating tension in other areas of your face.

Common Mistakes to Avoid

- Avoid applying too much pressure with your hands, which can stretch the skin and lead to premature wrinkles.
- Do not rush through the exercises; slow, deliberate movements are more effective for muscle engagement and relaxation.
- Ensure not to hold your breath during the exercises, as proper oxygenation is crucial for muscle function and overall skin health.

Estimated Time: 5 minutes for the complete routine.

Routine 5: Evening Relaxation and Muscle Relief Routine (< 5 minutes)

Purpose: To relax and relieve tension in the facial muscles, promoting a sense of calm and preparing the face for restful sleep. This routine is designed to reduce stress and minimize the appearance of stress-related lines and wrinkles.

Target Area: This routine targets the entire face, with a focus on areas prone to tension such as the forehead, eyes, cheeks, and jaw.

Step-by-Step Instructions

Starting Position: Find a comfortable seated or standing position with your back straight and shoulders relaxed. Close your eyes and take a few deep breaths to center yourself and prepare your facial muscles for relaxation.

Movement:

1. **Forehead Relaxation:**
    - Place your fingertips on your forehead.
    - Gently sweep your fingers outward towards your temples, easing tension in the forehead.
    - Repeat 5 times.
2. **Eye Relaxation:**
    - With your eyes closed, place your index fingers under each eyebrow.
    - Gently lift upwards and outwards to relieve tension around the eyes.
    - Hold for 5 seconds, then release.
    - Repeat 5 times.

3. **Cheek Relaxation:**
   - Place your palms on your cheeks with gentle pressure.
   - Perform slow, circular motions to massage the cheeks and release tension.
   - Continue for 30 seconds.
4. **Jaw and Neck Relaxation:**
   - Open your mouth slightly and massage the muscles along your jawline with your fingertips, using gentle circular motions.
   - Extend the massage down to your neck, focusing on any areas of tension.
   - Continue for 1 minute.
5. **Breathing for Relaxation:**
   - Inhale deeply through your nose, allowing your stomach to expand.
   - Exhale slowly through your mouth, releasing all the tension from your face and body.
   - Repeat 5 times.

Duration/ Repetitions: The entire routine should take approximately 5 minutes, with each exercise performed for the recommended duration and repetitions.

Pro Tips

- Ensure your hands are clean and warm to promote relaxation.
- Focus on maintaining a slow and steady breathing pattern throughout the routine to enhance relaxation.
- Use this time to let go of the day's stress and prepare your mind and body for a restful night.

Common Mistakes to Avoid

- Applying too much pressure, which can lead to discomfort or increase tension.
- Rushing through the exercises without focusing on the relaxation aspect.
- Holding your breath or breathing shallowly, which can counteract the relaxation benefits.

Estimated Time: 5 minutes for the complete routine.

Chapter 9

Progress Tracking and Motivation

Track Progress with Before-and-After Photos

To effectively track your progress with before-and-after photos, it's essential to approach this task with the same precision and dedication you apply to your facial exercises. Begin by selecting a well-lit, neutral background for your photos. Natural light works best, but ensure the light source is in front of you to avoid shadows that could obscure your facial features. Consistency in lighting, time of day, and location will provide the most accurate depiction of your progress.

When taking your before photo, position your camera at eye level and maintain a neutral facial expression. This standardization is crucial for comparing subtle changes over time. Use the same facial expression and camera angle for each subsequent photo. It's recommended to take photos from three angles: front, left profile, and right profile. This comprehensive approach allows you to observe changes from multiple perspectives, providing a fuller picture of your progress.

Wear minimal to no makeup in these photos to accurately capture your skin's texture, tone, and any changes in facial contours. Makeup can mask some of the subtle changes you're looking to document, such as reduced puffiness or increased definition in the jawline.

Set a regular schedule for taking these photos. Once a week is a good frequency as it strikes a balance between being able to see progress and not getting discouraged by daily fluctuations. Consistency in the day of the week and time of day you take these photos can also help minimize variables that might affect your appearance, such as morning puffiness or end-of-day fatigue.

Organize your photos in a dedicated folder on your computer or smartphone, and label each photo with the date and time taken. This organization will make it easier to review your progress over time. As you compile your photos, you might find it helpful to use photo comparison apps or software that allows you to view images side by side. This visual comparison can be incredibly motivating and provide tangible evidence of your hard work and dedication to the facial exercises.

Remember, the goal of these photos is not just to document physical changes but also to celebrate your commitment to self-care and the journey you're on to enhance your natural beauty. While changes may be subtle at first, over time, these photos will serve as a powerful reminder of how far you've come. They can also help you adjust your exercise routine as needed, focusing more on areas that may require additional attention.

Tracking your progress through before-and-after photos is more than just a means to an end; it's a way to visually document your journey, celebrate your successes, and motivate yourself to maintain your facial exercise routine. It's a testament to the power of consistency, dedication, and the transformative effects of facial exercises.

Progress Journaling for Success

Progress journaling emerges as a pivotal tool in the journey toward achieving a more defined jawline, reduced double chin, and overall facial toning. This practice transcends mere record-keeping; it serves as a tangible reflection of dedication, progress, and the nuanced shifts that occur over time. By meticulously documenting each exercise session, including the date, specific exercises performed, and any sensations or improvements noticed, individuals create a personalized roadmap of their facial shaping journey. This act of journaling fosters a deeper connection with one's self-care routine, transforming each entry into a milestone of achievement.

The significance of capturing small achievements cannot be overstated. These are the incremental victories that, when viewed collectively, illustrate the profound impact of consistency and effort. For instance, noting the slight but steady increase in muscle tone or the gradual reduction of puffiness around the jawline provides not only a source of motivation but also a reason to celebrate the journey itself. It's these observations that often go unnoticed in the mirror day-to-day but, when recorded and reviewed over time, reveal the transformative power of persistence.

Moreover, progress journaling acts as a motivational anchor during moments of doubt or stagnation. It's common to encounter plateaus or to feel as though progress has halted. However, flipping through past journal entries allows individuals to visualize how far they've come, serving as a powerful reminder of their capability and resilience. This retrospective view can reignite motivation, encouraging a continued commitment to the facial exercise regimen.

Additionally, journaling aids in the identification of patterns or correlations between certain exercises and visible results. This insight allows for the fine-tuning of routines, enabling individuals to focus on exercises that yield the most significant impact for their unique facial structure. It also provides an opportunity to adjust strategies in response to evolving goals or to address areas that may require more focused attention.

The act of writing itself also plays a crucial role in reinforcing goals and intentions. By regularly articulating objectives, challenges, and successes, individuals solidify their commitment to their facial shaping goals. This process not only keeps the end goal in sight but also embeds the journey into one's daily consciousness, making the practice of facial exercises an integral part of their lifestyle.

In essence, progress journaling is more than a mere exercise log; it is a narrative of transformation, a testament to the power of small, consistent actions leading to significant change. It encourages a mindful approach to self-care, where each entry serves as a building block towards not only a more sculpted and toned face but also towards boosted confidence and self-appreciation. Through the simple act of journaling, individuals not only track their progress but also celebrate their journey, making each step towards their goal an achievement worth noting.

Creating a Success Journal

Creating a success journal is an essential part of your facial shaping journey. It allows you to document your daily exercises and results, helping you stay motivated and focused on your goals. By keeping a record, you can easily identify what works best for you and make necessary adjustments to your routine.

To begin, choose a journal that resonates with you, whether it's a beautiful notebook or a user-friendly digital app. The key is to select something you enjoy using, as this will encourage you to make daily entries.

Each time you sit down to update your journal, start with the date and list the facial exercises you performed that day. This practice not only helps you keep track of your routine but also ensures that you are covering all target areas throughout the week.

Next, note the duration and repetitions for each exercise. This information is crucial for tracking your consistency and identifying areas where you may need to increase your focus.

After completing your exercises, take a moment to record any immediate sensations in your facial muscles or skin. Pay attention to areas of tension, relaxation, or increased flexibility. This reflection will help you become more attuned to the subtle changes in your facial structure and muscle tone.

In addition to written observations, commit to taking a weekly selfie to visually document your progress. Consistency is key, so try to take the photo under similar lighting conditions and at the same angle each time.

At the end of each week, reflect on your overall progress. Note any changes in muscle tone, skin elasticity, or facial contour. Consider how the exercises are impacting your confidence and overall well-being.

Based on your observations and reflections, decide if any adjustments need to be made to your routine for the following week. This could involve focusing more on certain exercises, increasing repetitions, or incorporating new exercises to target specific areas.

To make journaling easier, keep your journal and a pen, or your digital device, near the area where you usually perform your facial exercises. This way, you'll be reminded to log your activity right after your workout.

Be specific in your entries to track which exercises yield the best results for you. Use your journal as a motivational tool; on days when you're feeling less motivated, look back on your progress for encouragement.

Avoid common mistakes such as skipping journal entries, as consistency in tracking is key to understanding what works best for your face. Also, be mindful not to be overly critical of yourself. Remember that progress can be slow and subtle, so celebrate small victories and improvements.

Overall, dedicating just 5-10 minutes daily for journaling can significantly enhance your facial shaping journey and boost your confidence as you witness your progress unfold.

Motivation Tips for Consistency

Maintaining motivation for a consistent facial exercise routine can be challenging, especially when life's obligations demand your attention. However, the key to sticking with these exercises and seeing tangible results lies in cultivating a mindset that prioritizes self-care as a non-negotiable part of your daily life. To help you stay on track, consider implementing a reward system for yourself. This could involve treating yourself to a small luxury, like a relaxing bath or a new skincare product, after completing a week of consistent exercises. The anticipation of a reward can serve as a powerful incentive, transforming the exercise routine from a task into a treat.

Another effective strategy is to integrate facial exercises into existing habits. For instance, perform your jawline exercises while brewing your morning coffee or practice your cheek lifts during your evening skincare routine. By piggybacking these exercises onto already established habits, you're more likely to perform them consistently without feeling overwhelmed by adding another task to your day.

Social support can also play a crucial role in maintaining motivation. Consider partnering with a friend who shares similar goals. You can motivate each other by sharing progress, exchanging tips, and even practicing exercises together via video calls. This sense of community not only makes the process more enjoyable but also introduces a level of accountability that can spur you to stick with your routine.

Visualization is another powerful tool. Spend a few moments each day visualizing the positive changes these exercises will bring to your appearance and how they will enhance your confidence. This mental imagery can act as a motivator, reminding you of why you started and what you aim to achieve. Keeping a visual diary of your progress, as mentioned earlier, can complement this practice by offering concrete evidence of your improvements over time.

Setting small, achievable goals can also help maintain motivation. Instead of focusing solely on the end result, celebrate the completion of each exercise session or the consistency of your weekly routine. These small victories can provide a sense of accomplishment and encourage you to continue.

Lastly, be kind to yourself. There will be days when you might skip your exercises due to unforeseen circumstances. Instead of viewing this as a failure, treat it as a temporary setback. Acknowledge the effort you've already put in and gently remind yourself of your commitment to your facial health and appearance. This compassionate approach can help you bounce back more quickly and with renewed determination.

By incorporating these strategies, you can transform your facial exercise routine into a sustainable, enjoyable part of your self-care regimen. Remember, consistency is key to achieving lasting results, and with the right motivational tools at your disposal, you can maintain your routine with ease and confidence.

Long-Term Commitment Strategies

Building habits and maintaining long-term commitment to your facial exercise routine requires a strategic approach, focusing on incremental progress and the integration of these exercises into your daily life as seamlessly as possible. The key to success lies in creating a routine that feels less like an obligation and more like a natural part of your day. To achieve this, start by setting a specific time for your facial exercises, just as you would for any other important activity. This could be first thing in the morning, to energize and prepare your face for the day ahead, or in the evening, as a way to relax before bed. The consistency of timing helps to cement this habit, making it as routine as brushing your teeth.

Another effective strategy is to link your facial exercises with specific cues or triggers in your environment. For example, after washing your face in the morning and evening, proceed directly to your exercises. These cues act as a natural reminder to perform your routine, leveraging the power of habit stacking—where you stack a new habit on top of an existing one—to integrate facial exercises into your life without feeling overwhelmed.

The environment you choose to perform your exercises in can also play a significant role in fostering long-term commitment. Create a dedicated space that is inviting and conducive to your routine. This doesn't need to be a large area but should be a place where you feel comfortable and motivated. Personalizing your space with items that inspire you, such as motivational quotes, calming music, or even pleasant scents, can enhance your exercise experience, making it something you look forward to each day.

Tracking your progress is not only motivating but also crucial for long-term commitment. Beyond taking before-and-after photos, consider keeping a detailed log of your exercises, noting any changes in how your face feels or appears, even if they seem minor. This log will serve as a tangible record of your journey, allowing you to see just how far you've come over time. It's these small recognitions of progress that often provide the motivation needed to keep going, especially on days when you might not feel as committed.

Incorporating variety into your routine can also prevent boredom and maintain your interest over the long term. While consistency in performing your exercises is key, periodically introducing new exercises or modifying existing ones can keep your routine fresh and engaging. This not only prevents your muscle adaptation but also keeps your mind engaged, making each session a new opportunity to explore and improve.

Accountability plays a crucial role in maintaining long-term commitment. Sharing your goals with a friend or family member, or even joining an online community of like-minded individuals, can provide the external motivation needed to stay on track. These accountability partners can offer encouragement, share tips and experiences, and celebrate your successes with you, making the journey less solitary and more supported.

Finally, it's important to cultivate a mindset that embraces patience and self-compassion. Recognize that progress in facial toning, like any physical endeavor, takes time and consistency. There will be days when you might miss a session or feel like you're not seeing immediate results. Instead of being hard on yourself, acknowledge the effort you're putting in and the positive steps you're taking towards your goals. Celebrate the commitment you've made to improving your facial health and appearance, and remember that every exercise session, no matter how small, contributes to your long-term success.

By implementing these strategies, you can build a facial exercise routine that not only enhances your appearance but also becomes a cherished part of your daily self-care regimen, ensuring your commitment for the long haul.

Progress Log and Success Journal Template

Creating a structured and easy-to-follow progress log and success journal template is essential for tracking your facial exercise journey effectively. This template is designed to help you document each step of your progress, celebrate your achievements, and identify areas that may need more focus. By keeping a detailed record, you can visualize your improvements, stay motivated, and adjust your routine as needed to achieve the best results. Here's a comprehensive template you can use to start journaling your journey today.

Date: [Insert Date]
Time: [Insert Time of Exercise]
Duration: [Insert Duration of Exercise Session]

Exercises Performed:

- List each exercise completed during the session.
- Include repetitions and sets for each exercise.

Technique Notes:

- Document any adjustments made to improve technique.
- Note any feedback from videos or mirrors to ensure correct posture and execution.

Sensations During Exercises:

- Record any immediate sensations felt in the facial muscles during the exercises.
- Note whether any exercises felt easier or more challenging than usual.

Post-Exercise Feelings:

- Describe how your face feels immediately after the exercises.
- Note any areas of tension, relaxation, or increased circulation.

Visual Changes Observed:

- Document any noticeable changes in facial appearance, such as reduced puffiness or increased definition.
- Use this section to track gradual changes over time.

Overall Mood:

- Reflect on your emotional state before and after the exercise session.
- Note any changes in stress levels, confidence, or general well-being.

Skincare Routine Post-Exercise:

- List the skincare products used after exercising (e.g., cleanser, moisturizer).
- Note any changes or reactions in your skin.

Hydration and Diet Notes:

- Record your water intake for the day.
- Note any dietary choices that may impact your skin's health and appearance.

Additional Comments:

- Use this space for any other observations or thoughts about the day's session.
- Include motivational thoughts, challenges faced, or goals for the next session.

Photos:

- Attach or reference any photos taken to track visual progress.
- Ensure consistency in lighting, angles, and facial expressions for accurate comparison.

This template serves not only as a log of your physical progress but also as a journal reflecting your journey towards a more toned, defined, and confident facial appearance. Regular entries encourage a deeper connection with your routine, allowing you to celebrate every small victory and understand the importance of consistency and dedication. By personalizing this template to fit your needs, you can create a powerful tool that motivates you to stick with your facial exercises, adjust your routine as needed, and ultimately achieve your desired results. Remember, the key to success is not just in the exercises themselves but in your commitment to tracking progress, understanding your body's responses, and celebrating every step forward on this journey of self-improvement and confidence-building.

Thank You For Your Support!

I'm eager to know what you think!

Simply scan this QR code to jump straight to my book's review page on Amazon.

Your insights are invaluable – they aid in my growth as an author and assist others in discovering this book.

Feel free to share a photo or video review showcasing you with the book. Your experience could inspire others to embark on their adventure with my book!

Tessa Grimes

Conclusion

Final Thoughts: After 30 Days of Exercise

After 30 days of dedicated facial exercise, the transformation begins with subtle yet noticeable changes that collectively signal a rejuvenation of your facial contours. The initial signs of progress are often seen in the enhanced definition around the jawline and a reduction in the appearance of a double chin, as the targeted exercises work to sculpt and tone the underlying muscles. This period marks the beginning of a journey towards achieving a more youthful and toned facial appearance, with improvements in skin elasticity and firmness becoming increasingly evident. The commitment to daily routines pays off as the facial muscles become stronger, leading to a natural lift and sculpting effect that contributes to a fresher, more vibrant look.

The exercises designed to target specific areas such as the cheeks, neck, and forehead also contribute to a more balanced and symmetrical facial structure. With consistent practice, you may notice a decrease in facial puffiness and an overall slimming effect, which together enhance facial features and contribute to a more defined appearance. The benefits extend beyond the visible changes; many individuals report feeling a boost in confidence and self-esteem as they witness the positive transformations in their appearance.

Moreover, the integration of these exercises into your daily routine encourages a holistic approach to self-care, where the focus on facial toning complements other health and wellness practices. This period of dedicated effort not only yields physical results but also fosters a deeper connection with oneself, highlighting the importance of self-care and the role it plays in overall well-being.

As you continue on this path, it's crucial to remember that the journey doesn't end here. The foundation laid in the first 30 days sets the stage for continued progress and even more remarkable results over time. With ongoing practice, the full potential of facial exercises unfolds, revealing a more toned, sculpted, and youthful appearance that reflects your commitment to nurturing and caring for your face and skin.

Additional Resources

Skincare Products for Facial Exercises

To complement the facial exercises outlined in this guide, incorporating a targeted skincare regimen is essential for maximizing results and ensuring your skin remains healthy, resilient, and radiant. A well-curated selection of skincare products can significantly enhance the benefits of your facial shaping workout, aiding in skin recovery, hydration, and protection. Here are specific product recommendations designed to support your journey towards a more defined and youthful facial appearance.

Moisturizers: Look for formulations that boast hyaluronic acid, peptides, and ceramides. These ingredients are key for maintaining skin hydration, elasticity, and barrier function. A product like CeraVe Moisturizing Cream is ideal for providing long-lasting hydration without clogging pores, making it suitable for all skin types.

Serums: Incorporate a serum rich in antioxidants such as vitamin C or E, which can help fight free radical damage and support collagen production. The SkinCeuticals C E Ferulic serum is a popular choice that delivers environmental protection alongside improvements in fine lines, wrinkles, and firmness, offering a brighter, more even complexion.

Sunscreens: Protecting your skin from UV damage is crucial. Opt for a broad-spectrum sunscreen with at least SPF 30. Mineral sunscreens containing zinc oxide or titanium dioxide, like EltaMD UV Clear Broad-Spectrum SPF 46, are gentle on the skin and effective in shielding against UVA and UVB rays. This particular product is also well-suited for those with sensitive or acne-prone skin, as it helps calm and protect without adding greasiness or clogging pores.

Remember, the key to selecting the right skincare products lies in understanding your skin type and addressing any specific concerns you may have. Whether it's hydration, protection, or rejuvenation, each product you choose should serve a purpose in your overall facial care routine. By pairing these skincare essentials with your facial exercises, you're not only working towards sculpting and toning your facial muscles but also ensuring your skin remains supple, protected, and glowing.

Diet and Nutrition for Skin Health

Optimizing your diet is a crucial step towards enhancing skin elasticity and overall facial health, a goal that aligns perfectly with the facial shaping workouts detailed in this guide. The foods you consume play a significant role in nourishing your skin from the inside out, providing it with the essential vitamins, minerals, and antioxidants needed to maintain its firmness, elasticity, and youthful glow. To support the health of your skin, focus on incorporating a variety of nutrient-rich foods into your daily diet.

Firstly, hydration cannot be overstated in its importance for skin health. Drinking ample water throughout the day helps to keep your skin hydrated, plump, and full of vitality. Aim for at least 8-10 glasses of water daily, and consider adding hydrating foods like cucumbers, watermelon, and oranges to your diet, which are not only high in water content but also rich in vitamins.

Antioxidant-rich foods are your skin's best friend when it comes to combating the signs of aging and enhancing skin elasticity. Berries, such as blueberries, strawberries, and raspberries, are loaded with antioxidants that protect your skin from damage caused by free radicals and sun exposure. Green leafy vegetables like spinach and kale are also excellent sources of vitamins A, C, and E, which are crucial for skin repair and moisture retention.

Omega-3 fatty acids, found in fatty fish like salmon, mackerel, and sardines, as well as in flaxseeds and walnuts, are essential for maintaining skin's elasticity and preventing dryness. These healthy fats strengthen the skin's lipid barrier, helping to lock in moisture and protect against environmental pollutants.

Vitamin C is a powerhouse when it comes to promoting collagen production, a protein that gives your skin its firmness and structure. Incorporate vitamin C-rich foods such as oranges, kiwis, bell peppers, and broccoli into your meals to support collagen synthesis and enhance skin firmness.

Don't forget about protein. Lean sources of protein, such as chicken, turkey, eggs, and legumes, provide the amino acids necessary for collagen and elastin production, both of which are vital for maintaining the skin's elasticity and youthful appearance.

Lastly, nuts and seeds, including almonds, chia seeds, and sunflower seeds, are packed with vitamin E, zinc, and selenium, nutrients that protect the skin from oxidative damage and support its ability to repair itself.

By integrating these foods into your diet, you're not only supporting your overall health but also providing your skin with the nutrients it needs to complement the facial exercises in this guide. Remember, a balanced diet rich in vitamins, minerals, and antioxidants is key to achieving and maintaining the firm, toned, and radiant skin you desire.

Frequently Asked Questions on Facial Exercises

Many readers embark on their facial exercise journey with a mix of excitement and skepticism, often pondering whether these routines can truly yield the promised results. Questions frequently arise about the effectiveness, safety, and proper execution of facial workouts. Addressing these inquiries head-on can illuminate the path for those committed to enhancing their facial contours and overall skin health.

One common question is, "How quickly can I expect to see results from facial exercises?" The timeline for noticeable changes varies among individuals, depending on factors such as age, skin elasticity, and consistency in performing the exercises. Typically, with daily practice, initial signs of improvement can be observed within a few weeks. However, more significant results, such as enhanced jawline definition and reduced appearance of a double chin, may take up to three months of consistent effort. It's crucial to maintain realistic expectations and understand that facial sculpting is a gradual process.

Safety concerns also emerge, with many wondering, "Are there any risks associated with facial exercises?" When performed correctly, facial exercises are generally safe for most people. However, it's important to follow instructions carefully and avoid overexerting delicate facial muscles to prevent strain and potential formation of unwanted wrinkles. If any exercise causes discomfort or pain, it's advisable to stop immediately and consult with a professional. This is especially pertinent for individuals with pre-existing conditions or those recovering from facial surgery.

Another frequent inquiry revolves around the best time of day to perform facial exercises. The beauty of these routines lies in their flexibility; they can be seamlessly integrated into various parts of the day, whether it's a morning ritual to kickstart the day, a quick session during lunch breaks, or a relaxing evening routine before bed. The key is consistency, so choosing a time that fits effortlessly into one's daily schedule will help ensure long-term adherence.

Readers also often ask, "Can facial exercises replace cosmetic procedures?" While facial exercises can significantly improve muscle tone and skin elasticity, offering a more youthful and sculpted appearance, they may not replicate the dramatic results of cosmetic procedures. However, for those seeking a natural, non-invasive approach to facial toning, these exercises are an excellent option. They provide a sustainable method to maintain facial vitality without the risks and downtime associated with surgery.

Lastly, the question of combining facial exercises with other skincare routines surfaces regularly. Incorporating facial exercises into a holistic skincare and wellness regimen can amplify the benefits. Hydration, proper nutrition, and regular use of sunscreen complement the effects of facial workouts, enhancing skin health and resilience. Additionally, adopting a skincare routine that includes gentle cleansing, moisturizing, and the application of targeted treatments like serums can provide the nourishment and protection needed to support the skin's natural repair processes and optimize the results of facial exercises.

By addressing these FAQs, the goal is to equip readers with the knowledge and confidence to embark on their facial shaping journey, understanding the commitment required and the realistic outcomes they can achieve. With patience, dedication, and a comprehensive approach to skin health, the transformative power of facial exercises can be fully realized, leading to not only a more defined facial structure but also a boost in self-confidence and overall well-being.

Glossary of Terms

Antioxidants: Substances that protect the skin from damage caused by harmful molecules called free radicals. Commonly found in berries and green leafy vegetables, antioxidants play a crucial role in maintaining skin health and elasticity.

Collagen: A protein that gives the skin its firmness and structure. It's vital for keeping the skin looking youthful and is supported by vitamin C-rich foods and specific facial exercises aimed at enhancing collagen production.

Elastin: A protein similar to collagen that helps the skin return to its original position when it's poked or pinched. Lean protein sources contribute to the production of elastin, which maintains skin elasticity.

Hydration: The process of providing adequate moisture to the skin, both internally through drinking water and eating water-rich foods, and externally through skincare routines. Proper hydration keeps the skin plump, vibrant, and healthy.

Lipid Barrier: A protective layer of the skin that retains moisture and shields the skin from environmental pollutants. Omega-3 fatty acids, found in fatty fish and some seeds, strengthen this barrier, enhancing skin health and elasticity.

Muscle Tone: The state of partial contraction or tension in a muscle, even when at rest. Improved muscle tone in the face and neck, achieved through targeted exercises, supports skin tightness and contributes to a more defined facial appearance.

Nutrients: Essential vitamins, minerals, and other substances that the body needs to function properly. Nutrients like vitamin E, zinc, and selenium, found in nuts and seeds, are particularly important for skin repair and protection against oxidative damage.

Oxidative Damage: Harm to the body's cells caused by free radicals. This type of damage can accelerate aging and deteriorate skin health, making antioxidant-rich foods a key component of a skin-friendly diet.

Posture: The position in which someone holds their body when standing or sitting. Proper posture enhances muscle engagement during facial exercises and contributes to the overall effectiveness of the routines.

Skin Elasticity: The skin's ability to stretch and bounce back to its original shape Factors that support skin elasticity include hydration, a balanced diet rich in antioxidants and healthy fats, and regular facial exercises.

References and Further Reading

For those eager to delve deeper into the science and methodology behind facial exercises and their impact on facial aesthetics, a curated selection of references and further reading materials is provided. These resources offer a comprehensive understanding of the principles that underpin the facial shaping workouts discussed in this guide, enabling readers to explore the topic with greater depth and scientific insight.

1. **"Anatomy for Sculptors: Understanding the Human Figure" by Uldis Zarins with Sandis Kondrats** - This book provides a detailed exploration of human anatomy, with a focus on sculpting the human figure, which includes the muscles of the face and neck. It serves as an excellent resource for understanding the underlying structures that facial exercises aim to tone and define.

2. **"Facial Fitness: Daily Exercises & Massage Techniques for a Healthier, Younger Looking You" by Patricia Goroway** - Patricia Goroway's guide offers practical advice on facial exercises and massage techniques that contribute to a more youthful appearance. The book complements the routines outlined in this guide by providing additional exercises and insights into maintaining facial health.

3. **"The Yoga Face: Eliminate Wrinkles with the Ultimate Natural Facelift" by Annelise Hagen** - Annelise Hagen combines yoga principles with facial exercises to present a holistic approach to facial toning. Her book aligns with the philosophy of integrating facial workouts into daily life, emphasizing the importance of relaxation and muscle engagement for anti-aging.

4. **"Ageless: The Naked Truth About Bioidentical Hormones" by Suzanne Somers** - While not exclusively focused on facial exercises, Suzanne Somers' book delves into the broader aspects of aging and how hormonal balance impacts skin health and overall vitality. It provides a comprehensive look at maintaining youthfulness, which complements the goals of facial shaping workouts.

5. **Journal Article: "The Effectiveness of Facial Exercises for Facial Rejuvenation: A Systematic Review" published in Aesthetic Surgery Journal** - This scientific article reviews various studies on the effectiveness of facial exercises, offering evidence-based insights into how these routines can contribute to facial rejuvenation. It serves as a critical resource for those seeking to understand the scientific backing for the exercises recommended in this guide.

By engaging with these resources, readers can enhance their knowledge and application of facial exercises, ensuring a well-rounded approach to achieving a toned, youthful appearance that radiates confidence and health.

Printed in Great Britain
by Amazon

59050407R00086